My Night Terrors

A Life in the Dark and the Light

Margaret M.R. Mechler

My Night Terrors:
A Life in the Dark and the Light

"I did not banish the darkness,
I invited the darkness in."
— Margaret M.R. Mechler

"It only takes one person to show others what can be achieved.
The world moves forward the same way we heal — one step at a time."

— Margaret M.R. Mechler

My Night Terrors:

A Life in the Dark

and the Light

Margaret M.R. Mechler

A True Story

Published by Seal of Sarionae™

Published by Seal of Sarionae™
An Imprint of Margaret Mary, LLC

ISBN: 9781971169071

First Edition

Printed in the United States of America

This is a work of nonfiction. Names and identifying details have been used with respect and truth as remembered by the author.

Cover and interior design by Margaret M.R. Mechler

Sealed in love.

Protected in light.

Dedication

First and foremost, this book is dedicated to my husband.

You have walked beside me through most of this journey. You held me when I was falling apart and helped lift me back to my feet when I could not stand on my own.

It was you who helped pull me back to life the most.

For many years, neither of us fully understood the kind of love I truly needed, or even how to give it. But you never walked away.

You stayed.

You never abandoned me.

Through all the darkness, confusion, and pain, you remained beside me.

You showed me what it truly means to stand by the one you love, and what a real family bond looks like.

For that, and for so much more, I will always be grateful.

Acknowledgments

To the beautiful souls I call my *Butterflies.*

Jennifer J., Liudmila K., Lynn, Jazmine A., Melissa B., Wendy C., Nicole J., Debbie V., Elina, Aya and others who stood beside me during a time when I was finding my voice again — your encouragement, kindness, and protection helped me see the strength I had forgotten was there.

You reminded me that even in a world that can feel very dark, there are still people willing to lift others into the light.

For your support, friendship, and belief in me, I am deeply grateful.

Author's Note

This book is about healing generations of trauma, abuse, and invisibility.

It is for all those who have walked in darkness and suffered behind closed doors.

To the women of my lineage—my ancestors, my sisters, and those who cannot speak for themselves—I send you my unconditional love.

To the men of my lineage—my ancestors, my brothers, and those who carry their pain in silence—I send you my unconditional love as well.

Let us heal together through forgiveness, mercy, and compassion.

This is not condoning what has happened, but understanding that many suffer in silence and darkness.

— Margaret Mary Rose Witham Mechler

Prologue

A scream,

A yell,

A terror in the night.

One so small and innocent,

Should never have suffered such a burden.

The darkness had no end.

The light never seen.

The love never felt.

One by one,

Night by night,

The fear enveloped,

And the screams, the torment,

Terrified the innocence.

A never-ending Night Terror.

Part I

The First Fracture

"Sometimes the first break in our lives is the one that teaches us how fragile the world can be."
— Margaret M.R. Mechler

Chapter 1 - Sixteen

I was sixteen years old, deeply depressed and lost inside my own mind.
That was the first time I attempted to end my life.

Before that night, there were many small moments that had quietly shaped the way I saw myself in the world.

I grew up feeling like I existed somewhere in the background of my own family. I was not the oldest child, the one who set the example. I was not the youngest child, the one everyone fussed over and protected. I was somewhere in the middle.

My older brother was the only son, and in many ways, he was treated that way. Even when he made mistakes, there always seemed to be understanding waiting for him. My youngest sister had health problems when she was young, and because of that she received a great deal of attention and care from my mother.

That left my sister Melanie and me in a strange place in the family. She often felt like the black sheep. I felt invisible.

As a child, you don't always have the words to explain those feelings. You just notice things. You watch how people interact with each other. You notice who gets comfort when they are upset and who is expected to simply move on.

I remember watching my father spend time with my siblings and wishing, more than once, that he would spend that kind of time with me. It was not that he was cruel or unkind. It was simply that I often felt unseen.

Children do not usually say those things out loud.

Instead, they carry the questions quietly inside their minds.

Why do they love them more than me?

What did I do wrong?

Why am I not enough?

Over time those questions can grow into something much heavier.

By the time I reached my teenage years, I had spent most of my life observing rather than speaking. I learned to keep my thoughts to myself. I learned to hold my feelings inside rather than risk making things worse.

From the outside, I probably looked like a quiet teenager going through the normal struggles of adolescence.

Inside, however, I felt something very different.

I felt invisible. I felt unloved.

And when a young person begins to believe that they do not matter — that their presence or absence might not change anything at all — the darkness can begin to whisper dangerous ideas.

That is the place I found myself in at sixteen years old.

That night I swallowed an entire bottle of Tylenol. I know… it sounds foolish now. It wouldn't actually kill someone. But I was sixteen, naïve, and drowning in thoughts I didn't know how to escape.

The next morning, I woke up.

I told no one what I had done.

I got dressed for school like it was any other day. On the way, I stopped at the deli up the street from my house, then continued to school. I didn't speak to anyone. I wouldn't even look anyone in the eye.

Not until someone close to me asked the question.

"Are you okay?"

She was the only person I told what I had done.

Thankfully… she didn't keep my secret.

She dragged me straight to the nurse's office and told them everything. Within a short time, my mother arrived and immediately took me to the hospital. I spent the next few days there, with nothing to do except think about what I had done.

While I was there, I watched a young man playing pool in the recreation room.

And I remember asking myself a question.

"Why do I want to make them all happy by not being here anymore?"

That moment changed something inside me.

What I told the doctor and my mother during that hospital stay was only part of the truth.

But that was also the moment I learned something about myself that I had never known.

Something my mother told the doctor — something I could not remember.

Apparently, even as a very young child I had tried to harm myself.

Now, maybe some of those things could have been childhood curiosity. But my mother saw them differently.

"A child doesn't stick their hands into a toaster and turn it on from curiosity," she told the doctor.

"And what child puts their fingers in a light socket?"

There were other examples she mentioned that day. Those were simply the most dramatic.

I always wondered how I got the scar on my finger.

Then there was another word she used that I had never heard before.

Night Terrors.

She explained to the doctor that I had suffered from them nearly every night as a child.

I don't remember the doctor visits. I don't remember most of the terrors themselves.

And maybe that's a good thing.

Because if my Night Terrors have taught me anything over the years, it's this:

the human mind can create horrors far darker than anything written in fiction. I don't know exactly how this book will unfold, or how long it will become.

What I do know is this:

There are many people suffering from Night Terrors.

Not just adults.

Children.

Small, innocent children who face the darkness every single night while their parents stand helpless beside them.

If my story can do anything, I hope it shines a light on what those people are going through.

Let my voice…
my story…

be a light in the dark.

Chapter 2 - The Word I Never Knew

The first time I heard the words Night Terrors was during my hospital stay after my suicide attempt.

My mother mentioned them to the doctor as if they were something that had always been part of my life.

I remember sitting there confused, listening to them talk about something I did not even remember having.

That was the moment I realized there were parts of my childhood that other people remembered, but I did not.

For years I wondered, what is a Night Terror?

At that time, we had no computers, no internet, and we certainly didn't have cell phones. If we had, I might have found some understanding or clarity about what I was living through.

No one explained anything to me. I do not believe they fully understood what was happening either. They only knew that I would scream for help, thrash around uncontrollably, and wake up terrified.

My mother once told me that I refused to explain what I had seen in my dreamscapes. That is probably because, at the time, I had no words for what I was experiencing.

After all, how does a four-year-old explain drowning… or decapitation?

Some of the Night Terrors that I do remember were so graphic that even today some of them are difficult to explain. You see, I dream in full color. I feel, hear, and even smell within my dreams. My dreams are walking nightmares come alive, but inside my own mind.

This is the best way I can describe them today. Modern technology can now create movies that show things which once could only exist inside the mindscape or dreamscape. Technology has come a long way since the 1970s and even the 1980s.

Some of the Night Terrors I will share in these pages may be graphic or disturbing to some readers. I will attempt to give warning ahead of time. I am also including some of the less graphic Night Terrors so parents of children who suffer from them may understand a little better. Some doctors will tell you, "They will grow out of them. Don't worry."

I am here to tell you otherwise.

Many children who experience Night Terrors continue to have them into adulthood, but are afraid to speak about them for fear of being called crazy or delusional. Many creatives, artists, and writers experience vivid dream states but never realize what they are.

Night Terrors are not widely understood; however, nightmares are familiar to many people. The difference, at least from my own experience, is this: Night Terrors feel intensely real and can become life-threatening within the dream itself, occurring again and again. A nightmare may happen once or twice, but you wake knowing it was only a dream.

There were many times within these Night Terrors when I was being chased, and most of the time there was nowhere to run. Being chased was not the scariest part.

The scariest part came when I was caught.

Many years later I was watching the television show *Charmed.* In one episode, Phoebe was being chased in a dream by a masked version of herself. That episode changed one of my Night Terrors.

Not long after seeing that episode, I turned and faced my assailant within the dream.

I never had that particular Night Terror again.

I only wish that worked for the others.

For years I wondered, what is a Night Terror?

She told the doctor that when the Night Terrors happened, I would scream as if something was chasing me.

Sometimes she said I would sit straight up in bed, eyes open but not truly awake, thrashing and crying for help.

She said she would try to wake me, but I would push her away as if I could not see her at all.

When I finally woke up, I would be terrified and unable to explain what had happened.

After all, how does a four-year-old explain drowning… or losing their head in a dream so real it feels like death?

Chapter 3 - A Life I Don't Remember

As adults, many people can remember moments from their childhood. I do not remember anything prior to the third grade, and even some memories after that are difficult.

My mother shared the true story behind my premature birth with me after fifty years. This is the story she shared, and I must warn you; it is very difficult — not only for me, but for my mother as well. I do not know how she carried this in her heart for so many years. I will be fifty-six this year, and I only share this so you understand how long she carried this pain.

I was born on April 3rd, 1970, at 3:22 a.m. in Perth Amboy, New Jersey — three months premature. At that time, surviving a birth that early was rare.

My mother did not give me every detail of what happened to her that night, but I know it was not good. My biological father beat my mother so severely that he nearly killed both of us.

This was not the first time he had done this to her.

Less than a year before my birth, my mother had been carrying my brother Mark. He survived only a few days after birth and passed away on Mother's Day that year. Many of you can probably imagine the pain of losing a child on Mother's Day, and my mother still carries that pain even today.

Mom, I love you, and thank you for being an amazing, courageous, and strong woman. You taught me how to be strong simply by living every day. Many people would have given up, but you loved your children so much that you carried all of this pain by yourself.

This is how amazing my mother truly is, and the courage it must have taken.

Not long after my birth, the hospital sent me home with my biological father while my mother remained in the hospital recovering from her injuries and the major surgery she had undergone.

One night, my biological father wanted to go out drinking with his friends and left me and my older brother with his parents. They denied us as their grandchildren and rejected our lineage completely.

My grandmother reportedly said,
"You are no grandchildren of mine. My son cannot have children because he has a heart condition."

Not long after my biological father left, his parents placed my brother and me outside in the cold, in the middle of their driveway.

If not for a neighbor, who knows what would have happened to us.

This neighbor managed to get a message to my mother, who was still recovering from her surgery. She signed herself out of the hospital and came to rescue us.

Sadly, this would not be the last time we were left out in the cold.

Not long after my younger sister's birth, a year after mine, we were left homeless, hungry, and broke. I was told that my uncles came and rescued us that time.

At another point, my uncles came again in the middle of the night, hiding us until my mother was able to do what needed to be done.

After that, she was finally able to keep us safe.

I never knew my biological father. I grew up believing my stepfather was my father, and honestly, that is a good thing.

~

Many years later, after the birth of my own daughter, one of my biological father's brothers told me how my biological father died. Apparently, he was caught cheating with his brother's wife in their bed. He had a heart attack and died.

To this day, I still do not know exactly when he died or where he is buried.

I do have a few memories from childhood, but not many.

Now, I am left with the words of others.

Yet even though much of my earliest life exists only through the memories of others, small fragments have begun to return over the years. They do not come in order, and they do not always make sense at first. Sometimes they appear as brief flashes — a voice, a place, a feeling that suddenly rises to the surface. Other times they come through the stories told by family members, slowly filling in pieces of a life I could not remember on my own.

Memory is a strange thing. It does not always return when we ask it to. Instead, it waits until we are ready to face it.

And so, the pieces began to appear.

Part II

The Invisible Child

"When darkness becomes familiar, it begins to feel like home."
— Margaret M.R. Mechler

Chapter 4 - The Middle Child

Being the middle child was not easy.

I was not the oldest, so I was not the example. I was not the youngest, so I was not the baby.

Somewhere in between, I often felt invisible.

Looking back now, I can see how often I was blamed for things I did not do. At the time, I did not understand why. I only knew the feeling of being the one everyone looked at when something went wrong.

But there were also moments from that time that have stayed with me — small pieces of memory that somehow survived when so many others did not.

One of those memories is a yellow raincoat and matching rain boots.

I remember playing outside in the rain with the neighborhood kids. Back then, the manhole covers would sometimes spray water up like little fountains when the rain was heavy. To us, they looked like sprinklers.

We ran through the water laughing, getting soaked, not caring at all about the rain. I can still remember the feeling of the water splashing around my boots as we ran through those little fountains.

It was one of the simple moments of childhood that felt free.

Another memory that has stayed with me was the apartment we lived in after my mother escaped my biological father.

Apartment A-5.

I do remember the full building and even the neighborhood very clearly.

A-5.

Some memories stay with you in strange ways.

I also remember the day I had my ears pierced. Today, people get their ears pierced in shopping malls or jewelry stores, but back then it was done at the doctor's office.

After the piercing, I was told I needed to twist the earrings to help them heal. No one really explained how to do it, only that I needed to twist them.

One day I was twisting the earring in my left ear like I had been told.

Suddenly the earring was in my hand.

I did not understand what had happened. I was just a child doing what I thought I was supposed to do. But when my mother saw it, she became very upset with me. She yelled that the earrings had cost money and now my ear was ruined.

To this day, I still have a scar on that ear.

There were also moments that were simply frightening.

When I was young, I suffered from severe nosebleeds. One time the bleeding would not stop.

My mother rushed me to the hospital where they packed my nose and taped my face so the packing would stay in place. I remember the tape covering most of my small face.

When we returned home, my stepfather looked at me and said,

"You look like a skeleton."

I had no idea what a skeleton was.

I was only five or six years old.

What I do remember is how I felt.

I was scared.

That is something I have learned about memory. Even when the details fade, the **feelings remain**.

Even before I started school, there were moments that stayed with me in ways I did not fully understand at the time.

"The child I once was… still learning how to be seen."

Chapter 5 - The Night I Saw What Violence Does

As a young child growing up in an apartment complex, there were always other children around to play with. In our small town, we spent most of our time outside, gathering on the nearby fields to play softball or hardball until the day slipped into evening. I played softball, and I loved being part of a team. They placed me in the catcher's position behind home plate because I could throw to second base without any problem, and I took pride in that responsibility. I was always cheering for my teammates, always encouraging them, and because of that they gave me the nickname "Ego." It was never meant in a negative way. It was their way of recognizing that I lifted people up.

One year, at the end of the season, I received a trophy for Sportsmanship. I remember holding that trophy at the annual awards dinner, feeling proud of something that had nothing to do with winning or losing. It meant I had been seen for how I treated others, for how I showed up as part of that team. Even so, there was something missing that I did not yet have the words to express. My parents never came to watch us play. They had other obligations, other things that needed their attention. I understood that in the way a child tells themselves to understand, but I still looked for them. Every child does. Every child hopes to hear their parents cheering from somewhere in the crowd.

One night after a game, as we were leaving the fields that were practically connected to the apartments where we lived, everything shifted in a way that none of us were prepared for. What had been a normal evening filled with the sounds of laughter and conversation suddenly turned into something else entirely. As we approached the buildings, we saw a fight unfolding near our home. My father was sitting on the porch, just as he did every night, drinking his coffee and minding his own business. That was part of his routine, something steady and familiar.

A neighbor who lived across from us came toward him and began beating him without warning. There was no time to react, no time to understand what was happening. We were children, standing there, watching something we could not stop. Some of the older teenagers ran in to help, trying to pull the man away, but he was completely out of control. Later we understood that he was heavily under the influence of drugs, but in that moment all we saw was someone who could not be reasoned with and could not be stopped easily.

The situation escalated quickly. The police were called, and I remember seeing multiple officers trying to restrain him. It seemed like there were so many of them, yet even they struggled to get control of the situation. One of the teenagers had a baseball bat, trying to defend my father, trying to stop the attack. Nothing about that moment felt real, and yet it was happening right in front of us.

When it was finally over, my father was severely injured. Both of his arms were broken, along with other injuries that we were not fully talked about at the time. The physical damage was clear, but what followed was something I did not understand until much later. My father was never the same after that night. Today, I understand that he was suffering from severe PTSD, but at that time, there was no language in our world to explain what we were witnessing.

At night, we would hear him screaming in his sleep. There were times when my mother had to wake him because he was physically fighting while still asleep, caught in something we could not see. He was unable to work for a long time, which placed a heavy burden on my mother as she tried to take care of him and manage everything else in our lives. The stress in our home grew, even if it was not always spoken out loud.

That night left a mark on me in a way I did not fully understand as a child. I made a promise to myself, with complete certainty, that I would never take drugs, especially anything illegal. I had seen what they could do. I had seen how they could strip someone of control and turn them into something dangerous. At the time, that promise felt absolute. I believed it would protect me from ever becoming part of something like that.

What I did not understand then is that life has a way of testing the promises we make when we are young. Some lessons take years to fully reveal themselves.

My parents tried to take legal action against the man who had done this, but nothing came of it. There was no money, no compensation, no help with the medical bills or the loss of income from my father being unable to work. Eventually, that family was evicted from the apartment complex, but by then, the damage had already been done.

From the outside, we still looked like a family moving through everyday life. Nothing about us would have stood out to anyone passing by. But inside our home, something had changed. There were things that were no longer said, things that were felt but never explained. Experiences like that do not simply disappear. They settle into you, sometimes quietly, sometimes waiting for the moment when they rise again without warning.

Even now, I understand that what I witnessed that night was more than just a fight. It was my first real understanding of what violence can do, not only to the person being hurt, but to everyone who sees it and carries it forward.

Chapter 6 - Memories That No One Else Remembers

Sometimes the memories you believe to be true and accurate are denied by others. This is something I now ask myself with each memory that unlocks: Is this one true or not?

On one of my luncheon dates with my mother, I asked her if I had ever told her what my Night Terrors were about. She told me that I had been too terrified to even speak about them. Somehow our conversation shifted to my younger years in elementary school.

I asked her about the speech therapy I remembered attending because of my stuttering. She told me I had never stuttered—that my brother had been the one who needed speech therapy.

So now I question my own memory.
Is my memory lying to me, or has my mother confused the two of us?

I remember walking across the street with my teacher to see the speech therapist. I even remember part of one of the rhymes we practiced:

"Peter Piper picked a peck of pickled peppers."

I remember the therapist being kind and patient. I remember talking so much during those sessions that my throat would become sore. She would give me a lollipop afterward to help.

If I never went to speech therapy, then why do I remember it so clearly?

That was not the only memory I have that cannot be verified or denied.

There are moments from childhood that stay with you for a lifetime. Moments that quietly shape who you become.

I remember being a young child living in apartment A-5 when an elderly neighbor passed away. I remember watching as they took her away in a long black car. Today I know that car is called a hearse, but to a small child it was simply a car. In my mind, I believed they were taking her to heaven.

I was only four or five years old at the time.

The memory itself may not be perfectly accurate, but the feeling has never changed. I remember feeling a profound sadness. I may not have understood death then, but I do remember the ache in my heart.

I remember these things. Others say they never happened.

We lived in that neighborhood until I was sixteen years old. The second apartment we moved into was F-52 Bayshore Drive.

When I began elementary school, something unexpected happened. School became the one place where I felt safe. I loved going there. I hated the days when I had to stay home sick or when school was closed. Looking back now, that realization says a lot about how I experienced my childhood.

Another small memory returns to me from those early school days. Sometimes my grandfather would walk me to school. Instead of using the main street entrance, he would take me through a small alley that led to the other side of the school building. I remember holding his hand as we walked, feeling safe as we crossed the street together. These are the kinds of memories that come back to me now—small moments that might seem unimportant to anyone else, but to me they are pieces of a childhood I am slowly rediscovering.

Books quickly became my favorite companions. I loved reading Nancy Drew and The Hardy Boys. I could disappear into those stories for hours. Spelling was another subject I enjoyed and was very good at. Math, however, was another story entirely. Numbers and I never really got along.

Geography fascinated me. I would stare at maps and imagine traveling to faraway places. Sometimes I even imagined living in other time periods. I had forgotten that part of myself for many years.

One memory that stands out clearly is Arbor Day at school. Our class gathered on the front lawn as a new tree was planted. I remember Mr. Zamorski talking to each of us about the importance of protecting trees, flowers, and even the wildlife.

I remember creating turkeys using our handprints, coloring each finger a different color, and feeling proud of what I had made. I brought it home to show my mother.

But nothing ever went on the refrigerator. Nothing was hung on the walls.

Later in life, my mother pulled out a small book with my name written on the front. Inside were old report cards, schoolwork, and pieces of art I had created. She had kept everything.

That was the day I saw her love for me clearly.

She didn't want those memories to be ruined or thrown away. She wanted to keep them safe.

~

At school, things were different.

Teachers noticed when something was wrong. One teacher, Mrs. Stofski, saw that I was having trouble seeing the blackboard and moved me to the front of the classroom. When I got glasses and a couple of boys teased me, I never had to defend myself. The teacher stopped it immediately.

There were people in that school who cared.

I remember the school nurse, Mrs. Donnelly. She was always kind. I would often go see her just to talk, she understood how I was feeling most of the time, especially after my suicide attempt.

I'm sorry for jumping around these younger years, but I am writing this as the memories resurface. When I was in elementary school, probably five or six years old, I had my tonsils and adenoids removed, I remember waking up in a hospital crib so I wouldn't fall out of bed.

So once again, I find myself asking the same question:

Which memory is true?
Mine… or someone else's version of the past?

Another memory comes from that same period of my childhood.

I was very young, living on Bayshore Drive. I had been given a ballerina Barbie doll, likely for my birthday. Toys were precious to us then. We did not have many.

One day, I went to find my Barbie, and she was gone. I found my younger sister playing with it. When I tried to take it back, she began screaming and crying, telling our mother that I had given it to her.

That never happened.

But once the story was told, it became the truth everyone believed.

I never got my Barbie back.

Even as a child, I remember feeling how unfair that was. It was not the first time something like that had happened, and it would not be the last.

Years later, I would see similar situations happen again, even involving my own daughter.

When memories like this return, I find myself asking the same question I have asked so many times before:

Was I remembering it wrong?

Or was I simply the only one willing to remember it at all?

Not all of my memories feel uncertain.

There is one memory from my childhood that still fills me with a kind of joy that has never faded, no matter how much time has passed.

One Sunday morning, a large school bus painted in bright, vibrant colors pulled into our neighborhood. It stood out immediately, and like every other child nearby, I was drawn to it. We gathered around it, curious and excited, unsure of what was happening but eager to find out.

A young man stepped off the bus and began speaking with the parents. He was a preacher, new to the area, and he wanted to start something for the children—Bible study on Sundays.

And just like that, something new entered my life.

Every Sunday after that, we waited for that bus.

There was excitement in that waiting. When it arrived, we would climb aboard and be taken to an elementary school in a neighborhood we didn't know. It felt like an adventure, like we were going somewhere important.

Inside those classrooms, he taught us about God, about Jesus, and about the stories within the Bible. I remember learning the books of the Bible, repeating them until they stayed with me.

One verse stayed with me more than any other:

"For God so loved the world that He gave His only begotten Son."
John 3:16.

Even now, those words are still with me.

I had been raised Catholic, but this felt different. This felt like understanding, not just being told what to believe.

Brother Bill didn't just teach us lessons. He opened a door.

He opened my eyes to something beyond what I had been shown. He opened my heart to the idea that there was more than one way to understand faith. And without realizing it at the time, he opened my mind to a world much larger than the one I thought I lived in.

That stayed with me.

As I grew older, I began searching beyond what I had been taught. I explored different paths—Baptist, Christian, Jehovah's Witness—because those were the only ones available to me then. We didn't have access to anything beyond that.

But the curiosity had already been planted.

Many years later, I found Brother Bill again. By then, he had his own church, a family, and he was still doing what he had always done—teaching, guiding, helping others grow.

Seeing him again brought everything back.

And in that moment, I understood something clearly.

What he gave us was never small.

He didn't just teach lessons. He planted something that continued to grow long after those Sundays had ended. He helped shape the way I would see the world, the way I would question, and the way I would search for meaning beyond what I had been given.

And for that, I will always be grateful.

Chapter 7 - The Day I Asked for Water

There is one memory that has stayed with me for the rest of my life, not only because of what happened, but because of how I felt and what I learned without anyone ever using words.

At the time, we were living in the apartment on Bayshore Drive, F-52. My youngest sister was now with us, and although I do not remember my exact age, I know this happened after I had received my first pair of glasses. I had started wearing them in the third grade.

The kitchen was small, but bright in a way that felt almost overwhelming. Everything in that room was white. The walls were white, the cabinets were white, and even the light felt sharper than it should have been, reflecting off every surface as if nothing was allowed to remain unless it was perfectly clean. My mother did not tolerate anything that resembled dirt, and that room reflected that completely.

She stood there talking with my aunt Cindy. I do not remember their conversation, only that they were already deep in discussion when I walked in. Their voices moved back and forth between them as if I were not there at all.

I did not want to interrupt, so I stood quietly just inside the doorway, waiting for a pause that never came. My throat was dry, and I was thirsty. Such a simple need should not have mattered. Asking for water should have been easy.

After waiting as long as I could, I finally spoke and asked for a glass of water.

My mother turned toward me and handed me a glass of juice instead.

I remember looking down at the glass, then back up at her, trying to understand if I had said something wrong. I was not trying to be difficult or disrespectful. I simply wanted what I had asked for.

"I asked for water," I said quietly.

Everything changed in that moment.

Without warning, she struck me across the face.

The force of the slap sent my glasses flying, and I did not see where they landed. The sound echoed through the small kitchen, and for a brief second the entire room went still, as if time had paused long enough for me to realize something had just happened that I did not understand.

Then I realized my glasses were gone.

I dropped to the floor and found them underneath the kitchen table, reaching carefully, trying not to make another mistake, trying not to cause anything else to happen. My face burned where she had hit me, but the confusion stayed with me longer than the pain.

I did not understand what I had done wrong.

At that age, I was beginning to learn something I did not yet have the words to explain, but I felt the truth of it clearly.

Simply existing was becoming something I had to be careful about.

There is something else that needs to be said about that time in my life, because none of these memories stood alone. Each moment connected to something deeper that I did not understand then, but carried with me every single day.

With every one of these experiences, pain was present.

Not only emotional pain, but physical pain that lived in my body.

I remember the stomach aches more than anything else. Those aches were not occasional. A deep twisting sensation settled in my stomach and remained there, constant and unrelenting. There were nights when I lay in bed trying to fall asleep while that pain stayed with me, sometimes so strong that breathing felt difficult.

At one point, a babysitter told me to lie on my stomach and the pain would go away.

The pain remained.

The pain followed me through my childhood and into my adult life. Even now, there are moments when the same sensation returns with the same intensity. Doctors would later say stress caused that pain, but at that time I did not know what stress meant. I only knew that my body hurt, and I had no way to explain why.

Later, I came to understand that I was not the only one who carried that kind of pain. Stress moves through families, passing from one person to another even when no one speaks about it. The body holds what the voice cannot say. Silence carries more than words ever reveal.

~

Another memory from that time has stayed with me just as clearly.

That day had started out normal. I had gone to the movies with Jennifer, and back then the world felt safe enough for two girls to walk together without fear. We laughed. We talked about nothing important and everything at the same time. A lightness existed that only comes when childhood still believes life is simple.

I remember the anticipation more than anything else. The smell of popcorn, the excitement of choosing a drink, and the feeling that for a little while nothing else mattered.

I do not remember the movie, and I do not remember how I got home, but I remember what happened when I walked through that door.

The kitchen felt cold, not in temperature, but in a way that made something inside me tighten immediately. No warmth waited for me there. No comfort. Even now, I believe the season was spring, but the season did not matter. What I felt in that moment had nothing to do with the weather.

My mother closed the door behind me and immediately began yelling.

"You're grounded. Go to your room."

There was no explanation, no question, and no moment that allowed understanding. Confusion had already become familiar, but familiarity never made it easier.

I went to my bedroom, which I shared with my two sisters, and sat on the bed trying to make sense of something that had no explanation.

A few moments later, the door opened again.

My mother stood there, angry, and said, "Look what you did!"

Before I could respond or understand what she meant, she threw a broken ceramic piece directly at my face.

I reacted as quickly as I could, trying to protect myself, but I was not fast enough to stop what had already been set in motion.

The piece struck me anyway.

I remember trying to tell her I did not do it, even though I already knew the truth would not matter. She was not searching for truth. She needed someone to blame, and in that moment, I became that person.

She had made that ceramic piece herself, and it held meaning for her.

In that moment, I became the one who would pay for its loss.

After that, my memory becomes harder to follow, not because nothing happened, but because something in my mind stopped recording events the same way.

I remember the room clearly. The walls were pink, and everything in that space should have felt soft and safe, yet the room felt small and closed in. There was nowhere for me to go.

I remember seeing two beds, and even now that detail does not make sense to me because I had two sisters. I still do not understand where my youngest sister was or why I cannot see her in that memory.

There are gaps I cannot fill, no matter how much I try.

Pieces of that time feel as though they were never fully recorded. I can say honestly that I do not remember her at all during that period. Only fragments have begun to return, slowly, as if they were waiting for me to be ready.

When I look back now, one truth rises above everything else.

She believed I broke something valuable.

But she never saw what she broke in me.

This is another memory she says never happened.

But I remember.

~

My childhood was not made entirely of darkness.

There were moments when something else found its way in, moments where the weight lifted just enough for me to feel something different.

I remember my Uncle Bunny, Harold, coming over and gathering all of us neighborhood kids together. He would teach us games, simple things that filled the space with laughter instead of tension. We played hopscotch, handball, red light, green light, and so many others that required nothing except being present.

I remember him planting empty coffee cans in his yard so he could teach us how to play golf.

We did not have much, but in those moments, that did not matter.

Those were the times when the pain eased, not because life had changed, but because, for a little while, I was able to feel something else.

~

One summer, my mother took us school shopping at JC Penney's. I remember the heat outside, the kind that clings to your skin and makes the air feel heavy, but what stays with me most is what I was wearing and why.

I wore layers—more than made sense for that kind of weather. Sweatpants and coveralls weighed on my body, and I remember how heavy that fabric felt against my skin.

I was not dressing for the weather.

I was hiding.

I did not want to be seen. I did not want anyone looking at me, noticing me, or asking questions. Something inside me felt safer being covered, safer being hidden, safer existing in a way where no one could reach me. I did not understand that feeling at the time, and I did not have the words to explain it, but I trusted that instinct more than anything else.

When my mother saw me, anger came immediately. She did not ask why I was dressed that way or try to understand what I felt. Her voice rose loud enough that I knew others could hear, even if I could not see them. That alone made everything worse, because the one thing I had been trying to do was disappear, and suddenly I stood at the center of attention.

I stood frozen, not because I refused to answer, but because I did not know how. No explanation would have made sense to her because I did not fully understand myself. I only knew that I had tried to protect myself in the only way I could, and even that was taken from me.

I never saw those clothes again. They were simply gone. No conversation followed. No explanation. No acknowledgment. Over time, other things disappeared as well—clothes I liked, shoes, toys—anything that did not fit what was expected or approved. No one discussed those losses. Things simply vanished.

That was when I learned something without anyone saying a word.

Do not get attached.

Nothing was guaranteed to stay.

Looking back now, I understand something I could not see then. I was not only hiding my body. I was trying to protect myself in a world where being seen did not feel safe.

~

As an adult, I can now see something I could not see as a child. My mother believed fear and discipline were the correct ways to raise children because that was how she had been raised. She lost her own mother at sixteen and was sent to live on a farm where she had to work before she could eat. Her brothers were separated and sent to different homes, and my grandfather was rarely present because he was working away building bridges.

She carried wounds of her own, and I can see that now. I do not blame her, I understand her and I forgive her.

I will always and forever love her for the strength and courage.

Part III

The Shadows Grow

*"The darkness did not arrive all at once.
It crept in quietly, until one day I realized it had been living beside me all along."*
— Margaret M.R. Mechler

Chapter 8 - Always the One to Blame

I learned very early in life that when something went wrong, someone would eventually look at me.

The situation did not always matter. The truth behind what had happened did not seem to matter either. Blame would move through the room and settle on me as though that outcome had already been decided long before the moment even began. No one explained why. No one questioned the pattern. The role existed, and somehow, I filled that role without ever agreeing to that pain.

As a child, questioning that pattern does not come easily. A child accepts what adults say because no other reference exists. Adults are believed to understand more, to see more clearly, to know what is right. When blame is placed, a child looks inward and searches for a reason, even when no memory supports the accusation. Confusion becomes a quiet companion, and the search for answers turns inward instead of outward.

Over time, something begins to settle inside.

The change does not arrive loudly, and no single moment marks the shift. Awareness builds slowly in the background, shaped by repetition and strengthened by experience. Each moment adds weight, and that weight gathers until a quiet understanding forms.

When something goes wrong, no one will step in and defend you. No one will pause and ask questions on your behalf. No one will consider another possibility. You stand alone, trying to make sense of something that never made sense from the beginning.

When a child understands that kind of isolation, something within that child changes.

Some children become loud. Some children become angry. I became quiet.

Instead of fighting back, I turned inward. I began to live more and more inside my own mind, because that space offered something the outside world did not. Within my thoughts, I could question without being corrected, feel without being dismissed, and exist without needing to defend myself for things I did not understand. Silence became protection, and stillness became safety.

After a while, the pattern stopped surprising me. Blame no longer felt unexpected. Blame became something I anticipated, something I prepared for before anything even happened.

~

One memory from elementary school remains clear in a way that feels different from the others, not because the same pattern continued, but because for a brief moment, something shifted.

School was usually the one place where I felt safe. Structure existed there. Rules were clear. Adults paid attention in a way that felt steady and predictable. That environment created a sense of order, and order brought a kind of comfort I did not experience at home.

Even within that space, however, everything could change without warning.

There was a teacher we had whom the students secretly called "Hurricane Gadula." The name matched her nature. When anger surfaced, the change came quickly and without restraint, like a storm that moved through the room with force and no warning.

One day, that storm arrived.

I remember her anger rising, though the cause has faded from memory. What remains clear is the speed of the escalation. One moment we were sitting in class, and the next moment she grabbed a desk and threw that desk across the room.

The desk struck me directly in the chest.

The entire room fell silent. That silence did not feel natural. Every student seemed frozen, as though everyone present was trying to understand the same moment at the same time.

One of the students ran out of the classroom to get help. Within moments, the principal, Mr. Zamorski, entered the room and took control of the situation. His presence brought something unfamiliar to me.

Control.

Safety.

After that day, that teacher never returned to the classroom.

~

Moments like that remained with me, not only because of their intensity, but because those moments revealed something I had not experienced often. There were times when adults stepped in. There were times when someone chose to protect the children in the room. There were times when what had happened mattered enough for someone to say that such behavior was not acceptable. Those experiences stood apart from everything else I had come to expect, and because of that difference, they stayed with me in a deeper way.

Even so, those moments were rare. Most of the time, when something went wrong, I remained the one people looked at first. After a while, asking why no longer felt necessary. The question slowly faded, not because understanding had arrived, but because no answer ever came.

So, I adjusted.

I became quieter. I made myself smaller. I learned to stay out of the way, because somewhere along the line I had come to understand that being seen carried risk. That understanding did not arrive through explanation. That understanding formed through repetition and experience, through moments that taught without words.

At that time, I did not question any of this. I did not look at my life and wonder whether something was wrong or different, because growing up inside a certain environment shapes a single version of normal. No comparison exists. No outside voice offers a different perspective. No one explains that life can feel safer or more stable.

I believed this was how families lived. I believed this was how childhood felt.

Years later, after living through confusion, fear, and silence, clarity began to form. I started to see what I had not been able to see before. What I had lived through was not normal.

The moment that understanding arrived, something inside me shifted. The change did not happen all at once, and that shift did not remove the past or erase the pain, but that shift gave me something I had never allowed myself before.

I was finally able to stop blaming myself for things that were never mine to carry.

Chapter 9 - Living Inside My Own Mind

As I grew older, I became quieter, but quiet did not mean calm. Inside my mind, there was constant movement. Thoughts, emotions, questions, and sometimes anger moved through me without rest, building in ways I did not yet understand. There were moments when that anger rose to the surface and came out in ways that even surprised me, because I had spent so much time trying to keep everything contained.

One moment stands out clearly after my grandfather's funeral. My brother said something that struck deep, though I cannot remember his exact words anymore. What I remember is the feeling that followed. Without thinking, I picked up a plate and a fork and threw them directly at his face.

Another time, I kicked a wall so hard that I left a hole where my foot landed. At the time, I blamed myself for those outbursts.

Years later, when I was diagnosed with Bipolar II in my early thirties, I believed that diagnosis explained everything.

Now, looking back with clearer eyes, I understand something very different. Many of those moments were not random. I was often pushed, provoked, and antagonized until the pressure inside me built to a breaking point. When that breaking point came, my reaction became the only thing anyone saw, and in that moment, everyone could point at me and say that I was the problem. For a long time, I believed them.

But my life was not only anger and confusion. There was another world that existed outside of my home, and that world gave me something I did not realize I needed. That world helped save me.

~

I began working long before someone my age should have had a job. My sister and I worked at a local auction, helping vendors sell their items. One of those vendors sold porcelain dolls, and I spent many weekends helping sell them, but my fascination began long before I ever made my first sale.

Those dolls were delicate and beautiful, each one dressed in carefully sewn clothing, with painted faces that carried soft expressions. I spent much of the money I earned buying dolls of my own. One of them stayed with me long after those days ended.

Years later, I found a sketch I had drawn of her tucked inside a notebook. I had carefully drawn her face, trying to capture the softness in her expression and the curls of her hair. Looking at that drawing now, I understand something I did not understand then. Even as a young girl, I was trying to capture beauty.

"Some memories fade… but the feelings find their way back."

I was trying to hold on to something gentle in a world that often did not feel gentle at all.

My sister and I also worked weekends on my aunt and uncle's food truck. We were barely twelve or thirteen years old, but we loved working. For the first time, we had our own money, and we did not have to ask anyone for anything. That sense of independence meant more than I understood at the time, because that money gave me a small piece of control in a life where I often felt like I had none.

When I turned fourteen, I began working summer jobs. One summer, I worked at the school helping janitors clean and prepare the building for the next year. The following summer, I worked in the local public library, and that experience changed something inside me in a way I would not fully understand until much later.

That library was where I truly learned to read.

The librarian noticed my interest and began recommending books to me. I remember reading *Little House on the Prairie* and feeling as though I had discovered an entirely new world. Books became a quiet refuge. I did not simply read the words on the page. I saw them. The stories played out in my mind like movies, and the characters became real people to me.

That way of seeing allowed my imagination to grow deeper and broader, but for someone who experienced Night Terrors, that depth came with its own risks. I remember trying to read *IT* by Stephen King, and that book took me four years to finish. That experience taught me something important. My mind did not separate imagination from reality in the same way others might, and I began to understand that certain things were not meant for me to carry.

~

Later, the woman I babysat for helped me find my first real job at an Italian restaurant. She introduced me to the owner, and they trained me in many different positions. I stayed there for years, and during that time, I experienced something I had not felt before. The owners welcomed me as more than an employee. They treated me like family.

I loved working there, and in truth, I often preferred working to going home. The restaurant became a place where I could breathe. Through them, I learned recipes that I still use today. I remember one dish made from leftover spaghetti, mixed with cheeses and baked until the top formed a thick, golden crust. After it cooled, they would sprinkle powdered sugar on top. I never learned the name of that dish, but somehow, everything about it worked.

Those small moments mattered more than anyone probably realized at the time. They gave me pieces of a life that felt warm and human, and they showed me that another kind of life existed beyond what I knew at home.

During those same years, I discovered creativity. In high school, I took every art class available to me, including drawing, photography, and wood shop. I avoided cooking and sewing classes because I was determined that I would never become someone confined to a life I did not choose. I wrote poetry during those years, and much of that poetry carried darkness that I did not yet understand.

One time, my English teacher tried to pass one of my poems off as his own work. What he did not realize was that I had already shared that poem with my guidance counselor. That was how he was caught. At the time, I did not even understand the word plagiarism, but looking back now, I realize something important. There were people looking out for me, even when I could not see them.

~

One of my favorite pieces of art was a mural I painted on a wall in my high school. I painted a white African lion freehand against a black background, and the lion appeared almost ghostlike against the darkness. That painting remained there for a long time, and I wish I had taken a photograph of it. So much of life is only understood in hindsight.

During those years, I spent a great deal of time searching for somewhere I truly belonged. I searched for someone who would love me in the way I needed to be loved. In many ways, I was still the little girl who had never felt fully seen.

Even then, people my own age would come to me to talk or ask for advice. I never understood why they trusted me with their thoughts. Real friendships, however, were difficult for me to maintain. Before anyone could get close enough to hurt me, I often pushed them away first. Losing someone on my own terms felt safer than risking being left again.

At the time, I believed I was protecting myself. Looking back now, I understand that I was trying to survive in the only way I knew how.

~

Over the years, I held many different jobs. The auction, the food truck, the library, and the restaurant were only the beginning. Later, I worked in retail, fast food, and even in a bank that sold bonds. I worked for a small binder company where every person treated me with kindness and respect, and that experience showed me something I had never known before. Work could be something to look forward to.

Eventually, my path led me into transportation. Of all the jobs I held, driving a school bus became one of my favorites. I did not drive a regular route. I drove for class trips, band events, and special outings, which meant traveling to many places and meeting many different people.

One weekend trip to Wildwood has stayed with me all these years. There had been a mix-up between the bus company and the school, and they needed a driver for the entire weekend. Somehow, that driver became me. By that time, cell phones existed, so I called my husband and arranged for him to stay home with our daughter. The problem was that I had not packed anything. I told the band instructor I needed to stop for clothes, but we were already running late, so I decided I would manage with what I had.

On the way to Wildwood, the bus developed mechanical problems, and we had to wait for another bus. When we finally arrived at the hotel, something happened that I will never forget. The students, parents, and teachers had taken up a collection for me. They went out and bought two outfits and even a bathing suit so I would have something to wear for the weekend.

Those people barely knew me, yet they showed me a level of kindness that still brings tears to my eyes.

Moments like that began to change the way I saw the world. For most of my life, I had learned to expect the worst from people, but experiences like that showed me something else. People were capable of incredible kindness and compassion.

Looking back now, I understand that every job I held introduced me to another part of humanity. I met people from all walks of life, and without realizing it at the time, those experiences were preparing me.

Inside my own mind, I had built walls, but I had also begun building strength.

For a long time, I believed there was something wrong with me. I believed the anger, the outbursts, and the distance I created between myself and others meant that I was broken. That belief was easy to accept because those were the parts people noticed, the parts that were judged without anyone ever asking where they came from.

Looking back now, I see something very different. I was not broken. I was reacting. I was responding in the only way I knew how to a life that had taught me to stay quiet, stay small, and protect myself before anyone else had the chance to hurt me. The anger had a source. The distance had a reason. Every reaction had roots, even when I could not see them at the time.

No one asked why, and no one looked beneath the surface. Because of that, I learned to believe the same thing they believed.

That I was the problem.

It took many years for me to understand the truth.

I was never the problem.

I was a child trying to survive in a world that never felt safe.

Chapter 10 - The Night I Tried to Disappear

The night I tried to remove myself from life was one of the most emotional times I had ever experienced. By that point, I had spent years quietly collecting feelings I did not know how to express. I had learned to watch everything around me, noticing who received praise, who was given affection, and who was seen. I also noticed the silence that followed me, the absence of acknowledgment, and the quiet ways I began to believe that I did not matter. None of those moments alone seemed large enough to explain the pain I carried, but over time they built on top of one another until the weight became too heavy for me to carry alone.

I had spent most of my young life observing and hiding my truth. I saw my older brother and my youngest sister receiving affection, love, and attention from both of my parents. That left me and my sister, who was a year younger than I was, somewhere in the middle. She felt like the black sheep, while I felt invisible and unloved. At least she received time and attention from my father, something I prayed for more than once. My mother focused her attention on my youngest sister because of her diabetes, and she praised her only son.

By that time, my brother had become a young father after getting his girlfriend pregnant at a young age. Despite that, he was still praised. He would come home drunk, and the praise remained. I learned by watching and by listening, and I made promises to myself based on what I saw. I vowed that I would not get pregnant while I was still in high school, and I vowed that I would never take drugs of any kind.

Alcohol, however, was part of teenage life at that time, and there were several occasions when I became highly intoxicated. After each time, I told myself I would never do that again. After the third time, I finally learned my lesson. From that point forward, I limited myself, and even now I rarely drink more than one.

Returning to that night, I remember the feeling of being completely lost. I felt unseen, unloved, and unprotected. That combination is a heavy burden for anyone, especially for someone already moving through the physical, emotional, and spiritual changes of adolescence. I believed in God, Jesus, Mother Mary, angels, and guides. They were the only presence I felt I could turn to for comfort. Even now, I still walk with God by my side.

In Chapter One, I mentioned my first suicide attempt. There would be two more attempts later in my life, and I give thanks to God that none of them succeeded. My life has always carried a pattern where things seem to happen in threes. The following memory returns to that first night, but with more clarity and detail than I was able to share before.

That night, I swallowed an entire bottle of Tylenol, believing that action would end my pain. I was young and did not understand what that choice truly meant. Years later, I learned that what I had taken would not have ended my life in the way I believed. During the mid-1980s, there were no computers or internet to search for answers. Information came from libraries, newspapers, and word of mouth, and what I believed at the time was based on limited understanding.

The next morning, I woke up feeling disappointed that I had failed. At that time, failure felt heavier than relief. Looking back now, I feel something very different. I feel gratitude. This book would not exist if my life had ended that night, and everything I have come to understand about myself would have been lost before I ever had the chance to discover who I am.

That morning, I got dressed for school and pulled on a heavy sweatshirt so I could hide inside the fabric. I stopped at a deli, bought a buttered roll and a pack of cigarettes, and then walked to class as if nothing had happened. From the outside, everything appeared normal. Inside, I carried something no one else could see, something I did not yet understand how to speak about.

Later that day, during Phys Ed, a close friend looked at me and asked if I was okay. I told her what I had done. She did not hesitate. She grabbed my arm and brought me straight to the school nurse. That moment changed everything. I am grateful she did not keep my secret, because her choice saved my life.

Thank you, Lena. I love you for that moment.

My mother was contacted immediately and came to the school. She took me directly to the hospital. I remember the small room, the unfamiliar environment, and the bracelet placed around my wrist with my name printed across the surface. I played with that bracelet constantly, turning the plastic id over in my fingers until the material gave way and broke. They had to make me another one.

During my stay, I learned many things about myself, although much of that time remains unclear in my memory. What I do remember is the moment my mother spoke to the doctor while I sat in the room listening. She told him that when I was a small child, I would harm myself. She described how I would place my hand into a toaster and turn it on, and in that moment, I understood where the scar on my finger had come from. She also described how I would place my fingers into electrical sockets. The doctor suggested that behavior like that could be explained as childhood curiosity, but my mother believed something deeper was happening.

Then she said the words that would stay with me for the rest of my life. She called those experiences Night Terrors. I had never heard that term before, and at that time, I did not understand what she meant. Now I understand completely. My husband understands as well, because there have been many nights when he has had to wake me while I cried out for help in my sleep.

~

The next day in the hospital, something small happened that became far more important than anyone could have realized at the time. There was a pool table in the room and a bulletin board hanging nearby. While I watched someone play, my attention shifted toward that board.

Pinned to the surface was a large yellow smiley face, bright and simple against everything else around hanging on the board.

That image stayed with me.

In that moment, I made a decision. I was not going to disappear. I was not going to end my life to make anyone else comfortable. I was going to live. I was going to love. I was going to find a way to move forward, even if I did not yet understand how.

That decision did not suddenly change my life. The struggles did not vanish, and healing did not arrive overnight. But something shifted inside me. A part of me chose to stay.

Somewhere deep within my mind, a quiet voice began to rise, reminding me that my story was not finished.

For a while after that, I was okay.

But darkness has a way of returning when you least expect the return of that feeling.

Part IV

The Body Remembers

"The mind was protecting me from the trauma,
but my body never forgot."
— Margaret M.R. Mechler

Chapter 11 - The Memory My Body Kept

There were many things about my childhood I could not remember, yet memory is not the only place where the past lives. Some experiences do not stay in the mind where they can be seen and understood. Instead, they settle into the body, waiting quietly until something brings them to the surface.

Before I continue, I want to gently acknowledge something. Parts of this chapter may feel difficult to read. Not because everything is remembered clearly, but because some of what is shared was carried for me by someone I loved. If you have walked through anything similar, move through this chapter at your own pace.

I also want you to know this, with complete honesty and from a place I have fought hard to reach. There is light. I have found that light, and I share it now because I know what life feels like without it.

The first time the truth was spoken out loud, those words did not come from my own memory. They came from my sister. She spoke carefully, as though she understood the weight of what she was placing into my hands. I listened, but something inside me felt distant, almost disconnected, as if I were hearing a story that belonged to someone else.

My mind could not find the memories she described. No images surfaced. No moments returned. Nothing appeared that I could hold onto and say, yes, that happened. Yet something else responded.

My body knew.

For years, reactions had appeared without explanation. Moments of discomfort, fear, and confusion would surface without warning. Certain situations caused tension before my mind had time to understand why. Those reactions existed for so long that I believed they were simply part of who I was.

That conversation changed everything.

No memories returned, and no sudden clarity appeared, yet a new understanding began to form. A connection revealed itself between what my body felt and something my mind could not access. What had once felt random now carried meaning.

There is a difference between not remembering and never having experienced something. That difference revealed itself slowly over time. The mind protects in ways that are not always recognized. Doors can close without warning, sealing away moments that would otherwise overwhelm.

The body does not follow that same path.

The body holds what the mind cannot. Experiences remain stored in sensation, in reaction, in the quiet ways a person moves through the world without understanding why certain responses occur.

Looking back now, a clear truth rises. My body had been speaking for a very long time. I simply did not know how to listen.

There were moments when closeness felt uncomfortable, even when connection was desired. A simple touch could create a reaction that did not match the moment. Fear would rise without explanation, followed by confusion because nothing in conscious memory justified the response.

For many years, I believed something was wrong with me.

Those reactions felt like flaws, something to control or hide. Understanding had not yet reached the place where those responses began. My body was responding to something real, even without visible memory.

When my sister told me what had happened, she spoke about a time when we were very young. She described how we were invited to play games with older boys in the neighborhood. Trust came easily at that age. Inclusion felt harmless.

Somewhere away from view, those games changed.

She spoke of fear, confusion, and silence. She spoke of being told not to tell anyone, of being too young to understand, and too afraid to speak.

No memory of those moments exists in my mind.

That truth has been one of the hardest to accept.

For years, a search continued for those missing pieces. A belief remained that understanding would come if the memories returned. Clarity felt tied to recollection.

That clarity never arrived in that way.

A different kind of understanding took shape, one not dependent on images or recall. Trust had to be placed in what my body had been revealing all along.

My sister carried those memories for both of us. She held them, even when they were heavy, even when they caused pain. The weight of those memories showed in her, and I chose not to ask for every detail. Some truths do not require full description to be understood.

She carried them until the day she died.

That reality still lives within me.

A quiet form of grief exists in knowing that part of my story was held by someone else. Alongside that grief lives gratitude, because without her voice, understanding may never have come.

Even without memory, the impact remained.

The body does not forget.

Responses, protections, and reactions rise from experiences that once required survival. Those responses are not weakness. They are not failure. They are evidence of something endured.

For many years, attempts were made to understand those responses through logic. Explanations were sought. Diagnoses were accepted. Temporary clarity appeared, yet none of those paths reached the place where this lived.

This lived deeper.

Healing did not come from forcing memory or pushing for answers that remained hidden. Healing began when resistance ended and listening began.

That change came slowly.

Moments appeared where acknowledgment replaced doubt. Validity replaced questioning. Reactions no longer needed justification to be real.

Strength formed in that space.

Not the kind of strength that demands answers, but the kind that allows space for what remains unknown. Acceptance grew around the understanding that some parts of a story may never return in full detail, and that absence does not erase truth.

Healing does not always come through remembering everything.

Healing can come through learning how to live with what is felt, even when nothing can be seen.

Healing can come through trusting oneself, even when the story feels incomplete.

Healing can come through recognizing that the body has always carried truth.

Chapter 12 - What My Sister Told Me

The first time my sister ever mentioned anything about sex, we were teenagers. I remember the moment clearly, not because of the words themselves, but because of the way she asked the question. There was something behind her voice, something I did not understand at the time.

She asked me what I thought about sex.

My answer came easily, without hesitation, because my understanding was simple and untouched by anything beyond what I believed to be true.

"I wouldn't know. I've never had sex yet."

At that time, those words felt honest. They reflected what I believed about myself and my life. Looking back now, I can see that my answer did not match the deeper question she had been trying to ask.

That conversation stayed with me, even though I did not understand why. Only years later did clarity begin to form around what she may have been trying to say.

I was eighteen at the time and believed I was still a virgin. I had made a promise to myself that I would not have sex until after I graduated from high school, and I held onto that promise with quiet determination. Relationships came and went, but none moved beyond kissing and time spent together. There was no urgency within me, no pull toward something I did not feel ready to understand.

Sex, in my mind, carried weight. Emotional weight. Physical consequence. Meaning. A connection that should only exist when a person felt safe, understood, and fully ready to receive and give something so personal.

That belief remained steady.

The second time my sister spoke about the subject, everything changed.

That was the day she told me what had happened to us when we were children.

Even now, my mind does not hold those memories. No images rise. No scenes return. No part of me can replay what she described.

But something deeper responded.

My body remembered.

There is a difference between what the mind can recall and what the body continues to carry. The absence of memory does not mean the absence of experience. The body holds truth in ways the mind cannot always access.

The touch between two people who care for one another should feel safe. There should be warmth, trust, and a sense of protection within that connection. When trauma has existed, even when hidden beneath years of silence, the body reacts before understanding has time to form.

My sister's words stayed with me long after that day. I carried them quietly, sharing only small pieces with my husband, never allowing the full weight of that truth to be spoken out loud. A part of me hoped that if I searched long enough, memory would return and bring clarity with it.

That never happened.

My mind has kept those years sealed away, holding something behind a door that has never opened. Protection still lives there, whether I fully understand that protection or not.

The body, however, does not forget.

The nervous system carries experience in silence. Sensations remain. Reactions surface. Responses emerge without permission, without warning, and without explanation.

My body has endured many forms of trauma, and those experiences live within me in ways that do not require memory to exist.

There is a photograph that holds a different kind of truth.

Two little girls standing together, surrounded by wrapping paper and the remnants of celebration. Faces soft with innocence. Eyes open, unaware of what the world would one day reveal. A moment captured before understanding, before fear, before silence took root.

"My sister, Melanie. A part of me that never left."

When I look at that image, I do not see what happened. I see who we were before anything changed. I see trust. I see childhood in its purest form. I see two girls who believed they were safe.

My sister told me that when we were very young, around seven or eight years old, boys in the neighborhood would call us over to play games. We went willingly. Trust came naturally at that age. Inclusion felt exciting, something to be welcomed.

One of those boys was our older brother.

They would invite us to play hide-and-seek and other games that seemed harmless on the surface. As children, we believed we were part of something simple and fun.

We did not understand what was happening.

Away from the view of others, hidden behind bushes where the older children had created a space of their own, those games became something else entirely.

My sister spoke of fear. She spoke of confusion. She spoke of being told to stay silent, of threats that kept the truth buried. At that age, words do not exist to explain what feels wrong. Understanding does not exist to define what is happening.

Silence becomes survival.

I do not know how long those moments lasted. I never asked for every detail. She had already carried more than anyone should have to carry, and I could see the weight of those memories within her.

She carried them for both of us.

She carried them through her life.

She carried them beyond this world.

And even now, that truth remains.

Chapter 13 - Searching for the Truth

After my sister told me what had happened to us as children, more questions surfaced than answers. The most difficult truth to face was the absence of memory. No images came forward. No moments returned. Nothing within my mind reflected what I had been told.

A strange distance formed inside me. The story belonged to my life, yet I could not step inside of it. The past felt close and unreachable at the same time, like something seen through a fogged window where shapes exist without clarity.

For years, a quiet search continued. A belief remained that answers might appear if the right question was asked or if enough effort was placed into understanding. A part of me hoped that somewhere within my mind, a door existed that could still open.

That search led me into therapy. I met with therapists and psychiatrists, looking for guidance, hoping someone could explain what I felt and help uncover what remained hidden.

During that time, I received a diagnosis of Bipolar II disorder. At first, that diagnosis seemed to provide answers. Emotional highs, deep lows, anger that surfaced without warning, and periods of depression all appeared to fit within that explanation.

Even then, something did not fully settle.

My mind held no memory of those early experiences, yet my body responded as though those moments had been lived. Intimacy often carried discomfort instead of connection. Certain situations triggered emotional responses that had no visible origin. A sense of danger could rise within me without warning, even when nothing in front of me justified that reaction.

Over time, a deeper understanding began to form.

The mind protects in ways that are not always visible. Some experiences are placed beyond reach when facing them would overwhelm or break something essential within a person. Memory can be hidden, sealed away in silence.

The body follows a different path.

The body holds experience without needing conscious recall. Sensations, reactions, and responses remain, even when the mind cannot access the events that created them.

Years passed before my sister spoke those words to me. By that time, my daughter was already over ten years old. I was in my early thirties, building a life with the man who would become my husband. He stood beside me through moments that tested every part of my strength, offering support in ways that words can never fully describe.

The search for answers continued during those years. Therapy remained a constant presence. Appointments filled with conversations, questions, and attempts to reach something that remained just out of view.

The diagnosis of Bipolar II became part of that journey. At the time, the label was used to describe emotional extremes, from elevated states to deep depression. Language around mental health may change over time, yet the lived experience remains deeply personal.

Different approaches were explored in the hope that memory might return. Hypnosis was attempted. Techniques involving guided recall and visual stimulation were introduced. Each method carried the same intention, to reach beyond the surface and access what had been hidden.

None of those methods brought memory back.

A decision eventually formed within me.

I chose to stop searching for those memories.

Acceptance began to replace the constant need for answers. The understanding grew that some parts of my past remained protected for a reason that did not require full explanation.

My mind continues to guard those early years.

The body continues to remember.

One moment stands above all others in confirming that truth.

Years later, I underwent a medical procedure for pain management. The doctor prepared to inject medication into my spine. Anesthesia had already taken hold, and consciousness had faded.

According to the doctor, the procedure began normally. The first needle was placed, and then something unexpected occurred.

My body reacted.

The movement was immediate and powerful. My body twisted and turned with force, as though responding to something it recognized. The reaction was strong enough to stop the procedure entirely.

Afterward, the doctor spoke with both my husband and me. He explained that he had never witnessed a response like that before. The movement could not be explained by anything within the procedure itself.

That moment revealed something I could not ignore.

In my waking life, my body does not move freely. Stiffness has always been part of how I exist physically. My mother and my sister would laugh about that when I was younger, teasing me about my inability to dance or move with ease. My sister once tried to guide me, placing her hands on my waist and encouraging movement, yet my body resisted in ways I could not change.

Yet in that operating room, while unconscious, my body moved with strength and flexibility that I have never been able to access while awake.

No memory exists of that moment.

No conscious awareness guided that reaction.

Yet my body responded as though it understood something my mind could not reach.

That truth remains.

Chapter 14 - When the Body Speaks

One of the earliest memories of physical pain began long before any surgeries entered my life. Within my family, skin infections would sometimes appear, painful boils that my mother referred to as “bad blood.” As a child, I gave that experience a different name. I called it a curse.

One summer, before reaching ten years old, my mother took us to the beach with a friend of hers and her son, a place most people simply call the shore. At that time, a painful abscess had formed on my back. Instead of seeking medical care, my mother decided the wound needed to be drained.

Her friend held me down while my mother pressed against the abscess.

I remember the sound of my own screaming. The pain rose to a level that felt impossible to contain. Lifeguards ran toward us, believing something serious had happened. When the pressure finally stopped, my mother led me into the salt water, believing that the ocean would begin the healing.

A scar remained on my back for many years, lasting until my first major spinal surgery. Today, my back carries many scars, each one marking a moment when my body endured more than most people ever see. Those marks tell a story of survival, even when my body felt broken.

Before those surgeries, another moment changed the course of my life.

The birth of my daughter.

Her father entered my life during a time when I searched desperately for love. A deep emptiness lived within me, and I believed he might fill that space. We moved in together, and not long after, I became pregnant.

By the time the pregnancy reached three or four months, reality began to settle in. I spoke about needing groceries. I had tried to find work, yet no one wanted to hire a young pregnant woman. Responsibility fell entirely on him. Looking back now, warning signs appear clearly. At that time, fear shaped my thoughts as I tried to prepare for a child without stability.

He served in the Army Reserves and kept his gear stored in a spare room, the same space that needed to become a nursery. One day, something shifted. He picked up a broomstick and began swinging toward me.

Clarity arrived in that moment.

I said, "Hell no you didn't," and ran barefoot and pregnant to the nearest pay phone. The year was 1989. Cell phones did not exist, and escape required movement, not convenience. I called my mother, and she came to get me.

Once again, I returned to the same house where earlier wounds had been formed. Youth, inexperience, and lack of options left me with nowhere else to go.

My due date was February 7, 1990.

My daughter chose her own time.

She arrived on February 16.

Earlier that day, I went in for a stress test because the pregnancy had gone past the expected date. No one explained that labor had already begun. I returned home, ate a spaghetti dinner, and later that evening, discomfort began. With no prior experience, I believed the feeling came from something I had eaten.

My youngest sister recognized what I could not. She told me to go downstairs so my mother could begin timing contractions. As the intervals shortened, we left for the hospital.

When I arrived, I told the nurses my water had broken. At first, they believed the fluid came from my bladder. A closer examination changed everything.

The word "breech" echoed through the room.

My daughter was not positioned headfirst. She was coming into the world in a way that required immediate action. Today, humor allows me to tell her that she wanted everyone to kiss her behind on the way into the world, yet in that moment, the situation carried real danger.

A sense of calm settled within me. Somewhere deep inside, a knowing existed that everything would be okay. My mother felt the opposite. Fear surrounded her as the medical team moved quickly.

Surgery followed.

At 7:19 a.m. on February 16, 1990, my daughter entered the world.

The incision from that surgery still brings occasional discomfort, yet that pain remains manageable, a small reminder of the moment that brought her into my life.

Two years later, death came close.

Doctors later told my mother that my life had come within thirty minutes of ending. Illness began with symptoms that resembled the flu. My doctor confirmed that belief. When the condition worsened, I went to the hospital. The same conclusion followed, although X-rays were taken as a precaution.

I remember coughing thick mucus.

They sent me home.

Less than an hour later, pounding on my door shattered the quiet.

I was found lying on the couch, barely alive.

An ambulance returned me to the hospital. Quarantine followed. Heavy medication filled my system. A medical tent surrounded me as doctors worked to contain the infection.

The diagnosis was bacterial pneumonia.

My daughter was not allowed to enter the room because of the risk. My sister stood outside the hospital window holding her. A desperate need to touch my child filled every part of me.

The window would not open.

I broke it.

And I held her hand.

Life continued, yet challenges did not end there.

A few years later, a severe abscess formed in my mouth. At first, the pain felt like a simple toothache. Being born premature left me with little enamel, and dental problems followed me throughout my life.

The abscess burst, sending infection through my body.

Another hospital visit followed, accompanied by a dangerously high fever. Doctors eventually identified the cause and presented two choices. Their surgeon could remove my front teeth immediately, or I could leave and have my own dentist perform the procedure.

By the age of forty, most of my teeth were gone.

Now, at fifty-five, none of my natural teeth remain.

Later, after receiving a diagnosis of Bipolar II disorder, medications were prescribed to manage symptoms. Over time, those medications began to take a toll on my body. Weight increased rapidly. Health declined. Metabolic disorders developed. COPD entered my life. At my heaviest, my weight reached 396 pounds, and smoking three packs of cigarettes a day became part of my routine.

Looking back now, a painful truth emerges. A part of me may not have cared whether survival continued.

Eventually, that weight contributed to another injury. A fall through a broken couch caused severe damage to my lower spine. An orthopedic surgeon offered what sounded like a simple solution, a procedure that would burn the ruptured discs in my lumbar spine closed.

That decision became the worst mistake of my life.

Instead of repair, further damage occurred. The discs shattered beyond recovery.

A spinal fusion at L4-L5 and L5-S1 became the next step. Preparation included donating my own blood in case a transfusion became necessary. My family gathered around me that day, offering support in ways that had not always been present during earlier years.

After surgery, while sedation still held my awareness, confusion followed.

Hospital staff lost track of me.

My family searched through the building, moving from room to room, trying to find where I had been taken. My sister found me.

Relief followed, yet the experience left a lasting impact.

For a time, healing seemed possible. Weight began to drop. Strength slowly returned. For the first time in years, I joined kickboxing classes. Movement brought joy, and new connections formed with women who shared that space.

Then another injury occurred.

While camping with friends, my foot stepped into a groundhog hole, twisting my ankle in a way I had never imagined possible. By the time I reached the campsite, swelling had grown to three times its normal size, turning deep purple.

A boot became part of my life for more than two years while doctors searched for answers. A neurostimulator in my back prevented proper imaging, leaving the true cause unclear.

Eventually, a podiatrist recommended surgery.

That procedure never happened.

My sister spoke to the doctor, and the surgery was cancelled without explanation. Years passed before I learned of her involvement, and understanding never fully came.

While dealing with the ankle injury, pain developed in my sacroiliac joints. Injections and physical therapy brought no lasting relief. Another recommendation followed.

Fusion of both SI joints.

By that time, a neurostimulator had already been implanted to manage pain. Temporary relief gave way to another surgery when the battery failed.

Two additional major surgeries attempted to fuse those joints.

Both failed.

Pain reached levels that felt impossible to endure. Thoughts of ending that pain permanently began to surface during the darkest moments.

Doctors prescribed large amounts of medication, including morphine, oxycodone, nerve medications, and muscle relaxers. Another surgery to remove my gallbladder occurred somewhere within that timeline, one more procedure added to a long list.

Many other smaller surgeries took place throughout my life, yet those felt minor compared to everything else.

Even within all of that, a different truth exists.

Light exists here.

Life continues.

Today, morphine no longer controls my body. Smoking has ended. Weight that once felt impossible to carry has been released. Long walks with Max bring moments of peace and connection.

Pain still visits on some days, especially when my body is pushed beyond its limits.

Yet breath continues.

Strength continues.

Healing continues.

And for the first time in many years, my body and my life are moving toward something better.

Part V

The Night Terror Returns

"When the mind cannot face the truth in daylight,

the night finds a way to reveal it."

— Margaret M.R. Mechler

Chapter 15 - The Night I Remember

For most of my life, the past existed as shadows without form. My sister carried memories that my mind would not hold, and my body responded to experiences I could not explain. When I was nineteen years old, something shifted. Darkness returned, not as a story spoken by someone else, but as a lived experience that moved through every nerve in my body. That night revealed what true terror feels like.

My daughter was still a newborn when the Night Terror came back with a level of intensity beyond anything I had known before. These episodes had never truly disappeared. They changed over time, appearing in different forms and levels of severity, but that night crossed into something deeper, something far more consuming.

Describing what I saw and felt will never fully capture the reality of that experience. The vision centered on my newborn daughter, and what unfolded was something no mother should ever witness. I experienced the violent loss of my child with a level of clarity that erased any boundary between dream and reality. Every detail felt real because, within that moment, reality and dream became indistinguishable.

That kind of fear does not fade.

That kind of fear embeds itself within the body.

Even now, sensory fragments remain clear. A metallic scent filled the air. Steam rose from a manhole cover. Traffic moved around me with horns blaring, unaware of what was happening within my world. The face of the man responsible remains etched in memory. Those details did not disappear with waking. They became part of me.

After that night, fear of sleep took hold in a way that felt impossible to control. I began taking NoDoz to stay awake, fighting exhaustion rather than risking another experience like that one. My daughter never left my side at night. I brought her into bed with me, holding her close as I tried to rest. Sleep no longer felt safe. Sleep became something to avoid.

The terror did not come only once.

The experience returned again and again, reinforcing the belief that closing my eyes opened a door I could not control. Each episode strengthened the connection between sleep and danger.

Life began to shift around that fear.

Books by Stephen King disappeared from my hands. Horror movies became impossible to watch. Even conversations involving violence or fear became too much to tolerate. I searched for safety in lighter things, turning toward cartoons and anything that felt simple and harmless.

Even that did not always protect me.

Moments that should have felt safe could still trigger the same reactions. Something as innocent as Tom and Jerry could lead back into that same overwhelming space.

Before she passed, my sister shared something with me that I had never known. She told me that I spoke in my sleep. She would ask me questions, and I would answer her while still fully within those dream states. I never asked what those conversations contained. Some truths remain unspoken for a reason.

My husband has witnessed more than most people could ever imagine. Night after night, he woke me from screams that I could not control. Those moments were not rare interruptions. They became part of our life together, something he endured alongside me.

The Night Terrors reached beyond my immediate world.

Friends appeared within those experiences. Strangers became part of those scenes. Sometimes they were victims. Other times they caused harm. No boundary existed between who was safe and who was not. Even animals I loved appeared within those visions, placed into situations that no one should ever have to witness.

Within those experiences, death came in many forms.

I drowned. I fell from great heights. I was chased, hunted, and overpowered. An old belief says that dying in sleep leads to death in real life. That belief does not hold truth for me. I died many times within those experiences, and each time I woke again.

The terrors varied in intensity.

The vision involving my daughter remained the most powerful, yet many others carried similar weight. I experienced torture within settings that felt like England. I witnessed dismemberment in places that felt like France. I saw scenes that resembled Salem during the witch trials. People burned alive. People hanged. Bodies torn apart. Some were drowned, and survival led to further punishment, while death was labeled innocence.

History carries those events as facts.

What I experienced carried something deeper.

Fear of sleep became understandable within that reality.

Childhood adds another layer to that understanding. When Night Terrors begin at a young age, language does not exist to explain what is happening. A child experiences fear without the ability to define or communicate what feels real in those moments.

That child does not imagine.

That child lives through those experiences.

Those Night Terrors shaped my life for decades. They did not come occasionally. They remained constant, returning again and again, refusing to release their hold.

That presence remained with me for years.

All the way until 2024.

That year brought a change I had not believed possible.

The Night Terrors stopped.

A question naturally follows.

How does something that lives so deeply within the mind come to an end after so many years?

The answer came through a shift within me.

I finally saw the light.

Part VI

Learning the Darkness

"There can be no light without darkness.

When I finally accepted both within myself,

the fear began to lose its power."

— Margaret M.R. Mechler

Chapter 16 - The Year the Night Terrors Stopped

For most of my life, darkness remained a constant presence. The Night Terrors followed me through childhood, adolescence, and into adulthood, arriving each night with a certainty that felt as reliable as the moon rising in the sky. For many years, acceptance settled in, and I believed that this was simply the life I had been given.

In 2024, a change began.

The change did not arrive suddenly, and no single moment announced a miracle. The shift began during the lowest point I had ever reached.

By that time, my body had endured countless surgeries. My mind carried years of trauma, depression, and the weight of a Bipolar II diagnosis. Medications that were meant to help had taken a toll of their own, and pain had become part of my daily existence. Physical discomfort, emotional exhaustion, and spiritual emptiness existed side by side, woven into every part of my life.

One day, the weight of everything became too much to carry.

Physical pain pressed in from every direction. Emotional pain followed close behind. A deeper ache settled within my spirit, creating a sense of heaviness that could no longer be ignored. All of that pressure collapsed inward at once, leaving me feeling completely broken.

In that moment, something happened that had never happened before.

I screamed.

The sound came from a place deeper than anger or frustration. Words were directed toward God, toward the universe, toward anything that might be listening. I demanded relief. I demanded help. I demanded an end to a life that felt impossible to continue. A plea followed those words, asking for release if no help would come.

When the sound finally stopped, exhaustion took over.

My body collapsed into itself, curling inward as though trying to disappear. Movement no longer mattered. Time lost structure. Hours passed without awareness. Days followed without clear memory.

My husband left for work, unaware of what had unfolded inside me. Yet another presence remained.

My dog, Gracie, found me.

She stayed close.

Animals sense what words cannot express, and she did not leave my side. Her presence brought a quiet form of comfort that required no explanation.

By the third day, a change began.

The heaviness that had pressed against my chest for years felt different. Breathing became easier. The weight that had settled across my shoulders began to loosen. No sudden release occurred, yet a shift had clearly begun.

That afternoon, I stood up and took Gracie for a walk.

The walk extended beyond a simple trip around the block. Movement carried me forward, step by step, allowing fresh air to reach places within me that had felt closed for far too long. The rhythm of walking brought a sense of clarity, reminding my body that life still existed beyond the weight I had been carrying.

Something within me had changed.

The change did not feel dramatic or overwhelming. No clear explanation presented itself. Yet a quiet movement had begun within me, something that had been still for a long time.

Not long after that walk, a solar eclipse appeared in the sky.

As I stood outside watching that moment unfold, my attention shifted in an unexpected way. Shapes moved around the sun; forms I had never noticed before. Curiosity replaced the heaviness that had filled me only days earlier.

A question formed, and I began searching for answers.

That search led me somewhere I had not expected.

Videos of people painting rocks appeared on my screen.

At first, the images seemed simple, almost insignificant. Small stones covered in color and design. Yet something within me responded immediately. Each rock carried its own identity. Each color felt alive. Each design held a quiet form of expression that reached something inside me.

Recognition formed within that moment.

That night, I ordered acrylic paints.

The decision felt small at the time, a simple action without deeper meaning. Looking back now, that choice marked the beginning of something much larger.

A process had begun.

Healing moved forward quietly, without announcement, without urgency. Change unfolded in small ways, almost unnoticed at first.

As days passed, another realization came into focus.

The Night Terrors had begun to fade.

Sleep no longer carried the same level of fear. The darkness that once felt overwhelming no longer held the same power. Night after night passed without the familiar return of terror.

For the first time in my life, night became something different.

Night became a place of rest instead of something to survive.

Chapter 17 - Living With the Night

For most people, sleep offers rest and restoration. In my life, sleep became a battlefield.

Each night carried uncertainty. Darkness could return without warning, taking on forms I could not predict and placing people within those dreamscapes who sometimes suffered and sometimes caused harm. Some nights passed quietly, offering a brief sense of relief, but many others filled with chaos, violence, and fear so vivid that waking did not immediately bring peace. My eyes would open, yet the experience remained, continuing to move through my body as though the danger had never ended.

Living with Night Terrors for many years changes the way a person moves through life. Sleep loses its sense of safety. Approaching rest begins to feel like stepping into a place where danger waits just beyond sight. Caution replaces comfort. There were times when I tried to avoid sleep altogether. Caffeine became a tool. NoDoz became a shield. Remaining awake felt safer than closing my eyes and facing whatever might come.

The body, however, does not allow that resistance to continue forever.

Exhaustion builds, and eventually rest takes over, whether welcomed or not. When sleep arrived, the Night Terrors often followed.

My husband witnessed many of those nights. He woke me when I screamed or called out for help, pulling me back into a waking world that did not always feel much safer than what I had just experienced. My heart would race. My body would react as though a real escape had just taken place.

Memory remained.

The images stayed clear. The actions I witnessed remained intact. The sensations continued to move through me long after waking. Opening my eyes did not erase what had happened. Those experiences followed me into the day, shaping my thoughts, my reactions, and the way I moved through the world.

Carefulness became part of daily life.

Certain movies became impossible to watch. Certain books could no longer be opened. Even simple things, such as a cartoon or a news story, could introduce an image that my mind would later transform into something far more intense. Awareness became guarded. Every piece of information that entered my mind carried the potential to return at night in a form sharpened by fear.

For many years, a belief settled within me that something was deeply wrong.

Confusion grew alongside that belief. No explanation seemed to fit. No answer fully addressed what I experienced. The nights continued, repeating without clear reason, leaving behind memories that refused to fade.

Over time, understanding began to take shape.

The Night Terrors were not random.

Meaning existed within them.

My mind had been trying to process experiences that had never been fully understood or fully faced. Protection does not always appear as silence. Sometimes protection hides memory completely. Other times, protection allows fragments to surface through dreams, through fear, and through images strong enough to demand attention.

For many years, I did not recognize that process.

I endured those nights without understanding, moving from one day into the next while carrying exhaustion, fear, and caution. Life formed around those patterns, always aware that another night could bring something overwhelming and impossible to forget.

Without realizing it, each of those nights moved me toward something else.

A moment where darkness would no longer hold the same power.

A moment where the pattern would begin to break.

Time continued forward, and something within me slowly changed.

The nights that once controlled my life began to lose their grip, even before I fully understood why.

Morning eventually followed, even after the longest nights.

Chapter 18 - The Things We Carry

Grief does not disappear with time. Many people believe that time heals all wounds, yet that belief has never fully matched my experience, because time does not erase grief, grief changes shape. Some days feel softer and easier to carry, while other days arrive without warning and bring the same weight that existed when the loss first happened.

When my sister died, something inside me broke in a way that never fully repaired. The world continued to move forward, but a part of me remained frozen in that moment, holding onto a loss that could not be undone no matter how much time passed around me.

For a long time, I did not know where to place that pain, so I turned to the only place that felt safe, and that was my words. I wrote to her constantly, sometimes leaving a single message, and other times filling pages with everything I could not hold inside. I spoke to her through memories, through love, and through a connection that still needed somewhere to go.

Some days, even opening that space felt too heavy, because the weight of grief pressed too hard against my chest, while other days everything poured out all at once, including anger, confusion, and a longing that never seemed to quiet. Questions followed me during those moments, questions that had no answers and no one left to respond, yet they came anyway, rising from a place that needed to be heard even without resolution.

Over time, I created a quiet place in my home where all of those feelings could exist without explanation. That place became somewhere I could sit with everything I carried without needing to justify or explain any part of my experience. Her picture rests there, surrounded by angel figurines and small reminders of love, and beside her photo sits a picture of my daughter, because their lives remain forever connected. During one of the most difficult times in my life, my sister stepped in and helped raise my daughter, carrying a weight that did not belong to her simply because she loved us.

That kind of love remains, even after someone is gone.

That place holds more than photographs, because candles bring light into moments of remembrance, plants continue to grow and reach upward, and small objects rest there, each one carrying meaning and strength. Sometimes I speak to her when I sit there, and other times I remain silent, yet both feel the same because the connection has never truly left.

For many years, another feeling lived beside my grief, and that feeling was guilt. Looking back brings questions that never existed in the moment, especially when I think about my daughter and the times when both my sister and I tried to be friends to her when she needed guidance instead. That realization stayed with me for a long time, returning again and again as I tried to understand what could have been done differently.

Healing eventually asks something that is not easy to give, and that is forgiveness. Forgiveness for others and forgiveness for ourselves, because no one moves through life without making mistakes, and no one holds full understanding while living through each moment as life unfolds. Choices are made with the knowledge available at the time, even when that knowledge is incomplete, and looking back often brings a clarity that did not exist while those choices were being made.

Now, when I sit in that quiet place, grief no longer stands alone, because gratitude has found a place beside grief. I feel gratitude for the love my sister gave, gratitude for the memories we shared, and gratitude for the way her presence continues to shape who I am, even after her passing.

Along this journey, another kind of loss taught me something I had not fully understood before, and that came through the animals who shared my life. Some people see pets as companions, but those who have truly loved them understand that they become family, walking beside us through daily life and offering a kind of love that asks for nothing in return.

Over the years, I have said goodbye to many of them, and each loss left a space behind while also carrying a piece of my heart with them. Their time here is shorter, yet the love they give holds the same depth and meaning as any other connection, and through those losses I came to understand that nothing in this world remains forever, not people, not animals, and not even those who appear strongest.

Physical life has limits, but love does not.

Grief may never fully disappear, but grief no longer breaks me, because grief has become part of the path that guided me toward healing. Somewhere between grief and gratitude, a deeper understanding began to take shape, and that understanding showed me that love does not leave when someone leaves this world, love simply changes the way love remains.

"Still searching… even when I didn't know what for."

Chapter 19 - The Long Road Back to the Light

The memories of those changes remain clear in my mind, because that period marked the beginning of a shift I never expected to experience. While searching for videos to inspire my artwork, something unexpected drew my attention in a completely different direction. A speaker began talking about the afterlife, about souls, and about the possibility that life continues beyond what can be seen with the physical eye. What began as simple curiosity deepened quickly, and before I realized how far I had gone, I found myself immersed in something that felt both unfamiliar and strangely familiar at the same time.

I believe in giving credit where credit is due, because that moment marked the beginning of light returning to my life. Through the work of Michael Sandler and the Inspire Nation community, something inside me began to awaken in a way I had never experienced before. Alongside the steady support of my husband, my daughter, and my beloved Gracie, a shift began to move through me that could not be ignored.

“She stayed when everything else fell away.”

During one of his talks, he spoke about something called Automatic Writing. That idea immediately caught my attention, because I had never heard of such a thing before, yet something within me responded as though I had been waiting for that moment. The more I explored, the stronger the pull became, and I felt drawn to try the process for myself. A desire formed within me that went beyond curiosity, because more than anything, I wanted to reach my sister.

Her birthday was approaching, and that longing grew stronger with each passing day. If I could not speak to her in the physical world, then perhaps another path existed, one that I had never considered before.

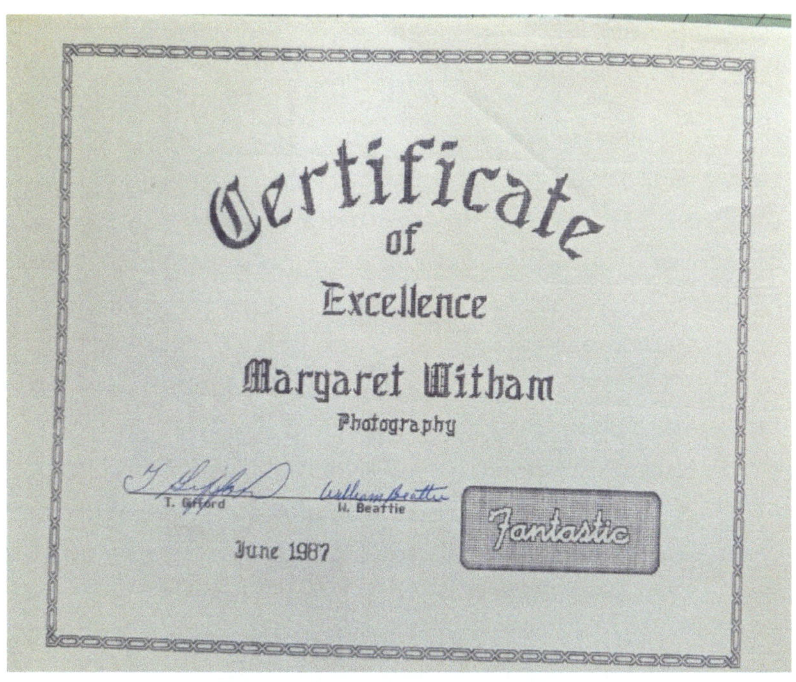

"Even then… I was learning how to see."

In July of 2024, I signed up for his AWE class, and he shared a prayer to use before attempting connection through Theta brainwave music, and I wrote every word carefully into one of my journals, even though I had owned many journals over the years that had never truly been used in any meaningful way until that moment, and something about this felt different, not in a way I could explain with logic, but in a way I could feel deep within me. During my first attempt, something happened that moved through me in a way I had never experienced before, because what came through did not feel like thinking, and imagination could not explain what unfolded, as images appeared all at once as though I were witnessing something rather than creating something, and those images carried a sense of reality without familiarity, leaving me unable to understand where they were coming from or why they appeared with such clarity.

Pyramids came first, yet they did not stand in a desert as one might expect, because dense jungle surrounded them, thick with life, as though those structures had remained hidden for a very long time, and the air itself carried a presence that felt ancient and alive. The imagery shifted without warning, and a great lion appeared, not carved from stone and not symbolic in any way I could dismiss, but alive, aware, and powerful, carrying a presence that extended beyond physical form into something that felt conscious and observing. The visions continued to move, and volcanoes erupted as fire and ash rose into the sky while the ground beneath felt unstable and alive, and then names began to appear one after another with clarity that could not be ignored, names I had never heard before and yet could not deny as they came through: Ashatara, Kalied, Shanara, and Palaedes.

Then everything vanished, and darkness stretched endlessly in every direction, not peaceful and not empty, but heavy, as though something existed within that space without needing form or visibility. From that darkness, another scene emerged, and I saw a vast desert that appeared still and silent, yet a massive shadow stretched across the land, far larger than anything that should have existed there, covering everything beneath a presence that felt unnatural and overwhelming. The images continued, and I saw what appeared to be crafts suspended in orbit around the Earth, silent and unmoving, existing in a way that felt beyond anything I had ever known, and then without warning, a brilliant white light expanded outward in a massive burst that felt overwhelming and impossible to ignore, a light that carried something deeper than brightness, something I could not define or understand.

Everything stopped.

I came out of that experience without answers, yet something inside me had shifted in a way that could not be undone. Some people might say imagination created what I saw, and others might call that moment a vision, but what matters to me is what followed, because at that time I still lived within the darkness that had shaped most of my life, and understanding had not yet formed, and awareness had not yet expanded, and I had not yet reached a place where connection, guidance, or protection felt real in any way I could trust.

All I knew was that something had opened.

Years earlier, I had made a conscious decision to stop watching the news, and my husband did not come home speaking about world events either, and that decision was never about avoidance, because living with severe Night Terrors teaches a person very quickly what must be protected, and I stepped away from that constant noise because my mind required protection in order to survive. After beginning writing and meditation, small changes began to appear, and at first those changes felt subtle and almost easy to miss, because the Night Terrors still came, yet something about them had shifted, and the fear no longer carried the same weight it once had, and slowly something began to happen that I never believed possible.

I started looking forward to my dreams.

Then one night became a turning point, because before going to sleep I wrote three simple words in my journal, I AM READY, and those words carried more power than I understood at the time, because in writing them I gave myself permission to receive and also permission to stop resisting what I did not yet understand, and a shift moved through me that I could feel in a way I had never experienced before. I was no longer the victim, and I was no longer the one being hunted, because something inside me stepped into a new place, and that place was awareness, and within that awareness I became the observer.

For most of my life, fear surrounded every experience within my dreams, and every moment felt like something happening to me that I could not control, yet that pattern broke in that moment because awareness stepped in where fear once ruled, and I remained present in a way that allowed me to see without being consumed, and that shift changed everything because awareness created space, and within that space something new appeared, and that something was choice. For the first time, I understood that my mind did not control me completely, and that space existed, and that control existed, and that fear no longer held the same power over me.

Dreams did not suddenly become gentle, and darkness did not disappear overnight, yet something inside me refused to be overpowered any longer, because I could observe what was happening, and I could respond to what was unfolding, and I could begin to change what came next. A realization formed slowly but clearly, and that realization showed me that darkness had never been stronger than me, because awareness had simply not been present before that moment. Night after night, my dreams continued to change, and fear loosened its hold while awareness grew stronger, and even Gracie sensed that shift, because she would lie at the entrance of my bedroom and watch quietly, as though standing guard while I slept.

Over time, another truth became clear, because I came to understand that I had control, and that my dreams no longer controlled me, and that realization changed everything in a way that could not be reversed. Light did not arrive all at once, yet light broke through in a way I could finally recognize, and even though some dreams remained intense, helplessness no longer existed within them, because I could step back, observe, and guide what followed.

As I write this now in March of 2026, moments of calling out during sleep have become rare, and when those moments occur, fear does not drive them, because a different pattern has revealed itself, and those moments tend to appear on days when physical pain reaches higher levels. As my mind settled, something else returned quietly to my life, and that something was creativity, and my daughter noticed that change before I fully understood what was happening, because what began with rock painting and handmade bookmarks expanded into something new when I came across a video of a man creating jewelry with copper wire, and that moment captured my attention immediately.

My husband had been scrapping that same type of wire for recycling, and I still smile when I think about how much of that wire quietly found a new purpose in my hands, because I followed the process step by step and began experimenting, and through that process I discovered something important, because I could create. Physical pain still existed within my body during that time, yet something remarkable happened whenever I entered what I now call creation mode, because pain would ease, and time would pass without awareness, and focus became so precise that everything else faded away.

Even my vision changed, because I would remove my glasses without thinking, even though I had worn them since the third grade, and despite being nearsighted, my hands moved with precision and ease, shaping delicate work without struggle, and that experience felt like a quiet miracle in my life. For many years, crocheting blankets had brought me joy until pain in my hands took that ability away, and that loss carried its own quiet grief, yet something new had taken place, because creation returned in a different form, and for the first time the meaning behind slow and steady truly settled within me.

When people ask how I moved forward, my answer remains simple, because I took one step at a time, and I learned to breathe, and I learned to pause, and I began living in moments that once passed by unnoticed. As physical movement returned, awareness expanded beyond my inner world, and one day while driving with my husband, I asked a question that surprised both of us when I pointed to a building and asked when that had appeared, and he looked at me with confusion because that building had been there for years, and in that moment something became clear in a way I could not ignore.

I had not been living.

I had been surviving.

That realization felt like waking from a very long sleep, and for the first time in more than fourteen years, I could truly see the world around me again. Another part of my life carried meaning that I had not spoken about until now, because for more than twenty years, games filled a large part of my world, including World of Warcraft, Diablo, and Rock Band, and after my sister passed, Rock Band disappeared from my life completely, because the last time we played together became the last time I saw her alive.

That day held laughter, music, and movement, just like so many moments we shared before, and earlier that same day I had driven her to a doctor's appointment, and as we stepped out of the car, she paused and said something that has never left me, because she told me she had dreamed of Aunt Mary and that she was going home soon, and at that time I did not understand what those words meant, and that memory did not fully return until after she passed. Many people say experiences like that happen near the end of life, yet no one prepares you for what those words truly mean when someone you love speaks them.

Looking back now, I understand something I could not see then, because that day was her gift to me, and she left me with laughter, and she left me with music, and she left me with love, and even now, as tears fill my eyes, one truth remains clear, because that day was not only goodbye, that day was her way of making sure I would remember how to smile again.

Chapter 20 - Learning to See

The changes did not arrive all at once, and no single moment announced that something within me had begun to shift, because everything unfolded slowly and quietly, in a way that made me question whether anything was happening at all. Around April or May of 2025, I began to notice something unusual in the way I was seeing, because my vision started to blur, yet not in the familiar way that comes with needing glasses or struggling to read something far away, and this felt entirely different, as though the change was not within my eyes themselves, but within the way I was perceiving the world around me.

Concern led me to the eye doctor, and I went searching for answers that would make sense of what I was experiencing, yet after the examination, I was told that my eyes were fine, and that answer should have brought comfort, yet instead, confusion grew stronger, because if nothing was wrong with my eyes, then why did my ability to focus begin to slip away, and why did simple things such as writing, working on the computer, or even playing games become difficult on certain days.

There were moments when I stopped trying altogether, because forcing focus only created frustration, and instead I would sit in silence and allow music to fill the space around me, and in the absence of visual distraction, everything else began to rise to the surface, because my thoughts became louder, my emotions became clearer, and something deeper began to move within me that I did not yet have the words to describe.

That period of my life felt like standing between two different worlds, because there were moments where light appeared, bringing clarity and a sense of peace that I had not felt in years, yet those moments never remained for long, and they would fade back into days filled with doubt, sadness, and a deep sense of self-judgment that had followed me for most of my life, because I had never learned how to love myself, and no one had ever shown me what that truly looked like.

By that time, my world had grown small in a way I had not fully realized until I looked around and saw what remained, because friends had drifted away, family had chosen distance, and silence had replaced connection, leaving only a simple foundation beneath me, which consisted of my husband, my daughter, and my fur baby, Gracie.

Gracie showed me something that no person ever had, because her presence carried a kind of love that asked for nothing and judged nothing, and every day she showed that love through the way she stayed close, through the way she looked at me, and through the quiet way she existed beside me without needing anything in return, and through her, I began to understand what unconditional love truly felt like.

Even now, the absence of that presence remains something I feel deeply, because the loss of my fur babies has left a silence that cannot be easily explained, and sometimes that silence feels heavier than the loss of people, because there is no confusion in the love they give, and when that love is gone, the emptiness that follows carries a weight that settles deep within the heart.

Loss became something familiar in my life, because over the years I have stood at the exact moments when people leave this world, and I have witnessed the shift that takes place when the light leaves their eyes, and I saw that moment with my Uncle Butchie, with a friend's father in a hospital room, and with my father-in-law, and each time there was a change that could be felt even when no words were spoken, because something essential had moved on.

In those moments, I found myself doing something I did not fully understand at the time, because I gave them permission to go, sometimes speaking the words out loud and other times whispering them quietly so only they could hear, telling them that they could go home and that their time here had come to an end, and I did the same for my father, even though I was not physically present at the exact moment he passed, because the words had already been spoken, and a few days later, he was gone.

Experiences like those do not fade, because they settle into the heart and begin to shape the way life and death are understood, and over time, those moments began to connect with the changes that were already unfolding within me.

In August of 2025, another layer of understanding began to open when I was introduced to something known as the Architect through Robert Edward Grant, and what began as curiosity slowly turned into something deeper, because I wanted to understand what I was seeing, what I was feeling, and why everything within and around me seemed to be shifting in ways that could not be explained through logic alone.

Through that experience, I began to relearn how to see, not only with my eyes, but with awareness, and as that awareness grew, patterns began to appear, symbols began to stand out, and meanings began to form in ways I had never recognized before, yet what I came to understand mattered far more than any symbol itself.

Meaning is not universal.

Meaning is personal.

A dove may represent peace to one person, while to another person, that same image holds no deeper meaning at all, and understanding this shifted something important within me, because I began to see that every person views the world through their own experiences, their own emotions, and their own level of awareness, and no single interpretation holds authority over another.

That realization changed the way I saw people, because I stopped focusing only on who someone appeared to be on the surface, and instead began to recognize who that person could become, and something deeper began to reveal itself beyond appearance and behavior.

I began to see the soul beneath the person.

That awareness allowed me to step back instead of reacting, to widen my perspective instead of becoming overwhelmed, and to observe without immediately placing judgment on what I was seeing, and through that process, something became clear.

The world had not changed.

The way I saw the world had changed.

And once that shift takes place, there is no returning to the way things once appeared.

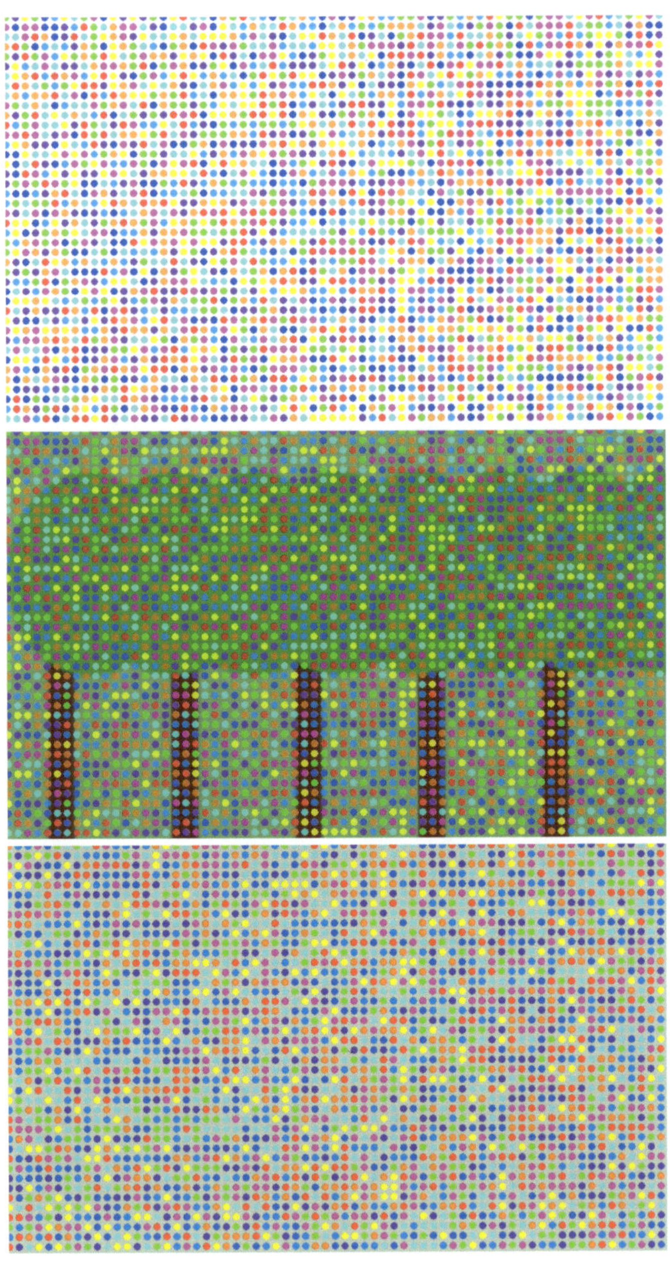

"The world didn't change… the way I see it did."

Chapter 21 - What My Eyes Began to See

During my healing, another layer of experience began to unfold, one that has been difficult to explain, not because the experience lacks meaning, but because language does not easily hold what I have been living through. Even now, I search for words that do not distort what I am trying to share, because my intention is not to impress anyone, but to be understood in a way that feels honest and whole.

After coming off long-term morphine under careful medical supervision, a change began within my vision that could not be ignored, and this change did not resemble anything familiar such as needing stronger glasses or adjusting to light sensitivity, because the shift occurred within the way my brain processed what I was seeing rather than within my eyes themselves. At first, the change appeared subtle, almost easy to dismiss, but once awareness settled in, there was no returning to the way I had seen before.

Across my entire field of vision, tiny points of color began to appear, each one small and precise, like a pinprick of light that remained steady and unmoving. These points do not drift or pulse, and they do not organize into patterns, yet they remain constant and present whether my eyes are open or closed, forming a field that exists independent of anything else I see.

I have spent long periods of time observing them quietly, allowing myself to see without forcing meaning onto what is present, and through that observation I have come to understand that the structure remains consistent while the intensity changes. At times, one color becomes more vivid than the others, standing out sharply, while at other times either white or black becomes more dominant depending on whether my eyes are open or closed. When my body grows tired, the intensity increases, and those points begin to dominate my vision to such a degree that seeing clearly becomes difficult, and during those moments I rely more on memory and spatial awareness than direct sight.

The points themselves do not form images, and they do not move, because the images come from somewhere else entirely, and over time I have learned to recognize when that shift is about to occur. When my eyes are open, a subtle blurring begins to form, and that blurring acts as a signal, letting me know that something is about to appear more clearly once I close my eyes. When my eyes close, detail increases, and shapes begin to form, followed by symbols and images that feel separate from the constant field of color.

There is always a sense of arrival.

That feeling cannot be easily explained, yet once experienced, recognition becomes immediate and undeniable. I do not chase what appears, and I do not attempt to hold onto anything that forms, because I observe what comes forward and allow each image to fade in its own time.

Alongside these visual changes, my body began to respond in ways that carried equal intensity. Waves of heat would move through me without warning, rising quickly and spreading through my body before fading, similar to a hot flash yet distinct in the way the sensation moved and settled. At other times, vibrations would begin subtly and then build, moving through my body with increasing strength until my full attention became focused on what I was feeling.

The most intense sensations came in the form of what can best be described as electrical surges, beginning in my spine and traveling downward through my hips and into my legs, with a strength that felt similar to a TENS unit turned to the highest setting, strong enough to demand complete awareness and at times strong enough to bring pain that made rest difficult.

These experiences most often appeared at night.

During the day, movement softened their presence, because activity allowed my body to distribute the sensation in a way that kept everything in the background, yet at night, when stillness settled in and distraction disappeared, those sensations came forward fully, and I felt everything with an intensity that is difficult to explain to anyone who has never lived through something similar.

There were many nights when sleep would not come, not because exhaustion was absent, but because my body would not settle into rest, and over time I began searching for ways to support myself through those moments. I discovered that a simple combination helped ease the intensity, and that combination consisted of a glass of water, a pinch of salt, and a teaspoon of honey, and while I cannot explain exactly why this worked, I know through experience that the effect was real.

The salt supported my system, the water grounded my body, and the honey brought a sense of calm that allowed the intensity to soften. The sensations would ease, my body would begin to settle, and rest would eventually follow.

This is not something that happens occasionally.

This is something I live with daily.

No part of this path was something I chose, yet I have chosen how I respond, because I observe what is happening without allowing fear to take control, and I remain aware of my body without forcing meaning onto every image or sensation that arises. Each experience is allowed to come and go in its own time, without chasing and without resistance.

This approach did not begin here.

This approach was built through years of learning how to live with my dreams and how to live with pain, and now that same awareness has become part of another layer of my life that requires patience, presence, and acceptance.

And as with everything that has come before, I continue forward.

One moment at a time.

Epilogue - Becoming Whole

If you have made it this far in my story, then you have walked beside me through darkness, through Night Terrors, through grief, through loss, through confusion, and through years where I believed I might never find my way out of the shadows that lived within my own mind, and yet you have also witnessed something else unfolding alongside that darkness, because you have seen that healing exists, not as something reserved for a chosen few, but as something that becomes possible through movement, through persistence, and through the quiet decision to take another step forward even when the path ahead cannot be seen clearly.

Healing did not arrive in a single moment, and no perfect realization suddenly made everything make sense, because the path formed slowly, shaped by each step I chose to take even when the weight of everything behind me felt too heavy to carry, and through that movement, something began to change, because healing does not come all at once, and healing does not demand perfection, but instead grows through moments that build upon one another until a life begins to form again, breath by breath, step by step, until one day awareness arrives and shows that distance has been traveled, even when progress once felt invisible.

If my story offers anything, I hope that understanding reaches you in a way that feels real, because no matter how deep the darkness has been, no matter how heavy the nights have felt, something within you remains untouched, something within you has never been lost, even if that part feels buried, distant, or unreachable, because that part still exists, waiting patiently, waiting without judgment, waiting for the moment when you are ready to turn toward your own light.

The path toward that light may take time, and the journey may require strength that feels beyond reach, and moments may arise that ask you to face things you would rather leave behind, yet that part within you remains, steady and present, and I know this because I found my way back, not in a perfect way and not in a single moment, but enough to continue forward, enough to keep moving, enough to begin seeing something I had never truly seen before.

I began to see.

Not only the world around me, but the souls who move within that world, and in that seeing, the smallest moments began to return, the quiet moments that once passed unnoticed, the way morning greets the body when eyes first open, the stillness that settles before sleep arrives, the breath that moves steadily through the body without asking for anything in return, and within those moments, something new took root.

Gratitude.

Not forced, not practiced, not something I had to remind myself to feel, but something that exists naturally within the act of living, within the simple awareness of being present, within the recognition that each breath carries life forward.

Laughter found a place in my life again, not the kind that must be searched for or created, but the kind that rises freely from within and moves outward, touching everything around me, and that joy no longer feels separate from who I am, because that joy has become something I carry, something that flows through me and reaches others in ways I may never fully see, yet I know that connection exists.

The way I see people has changed as well, because I no longer look only at who someone appears to be, but I recognize who that person can become, and I see beyond the pain, beyond the fear, beyond the brokenness, because I have come to understand that something deeper exists beneath all of that, something that remains whole even when everything else feels fractured.

That understanding has changed the way I move through this world.

I no longer walk alone.

I walk with my Father, God our Creator, and I walk with Yeshua as my brother, and I walk with Mother Mary and my sister Mary Magdalena, and I walk with Archangel Michael and the rest of my Dream Team, who guide me, protect me, and love me in ways that once felt impossible to understand and now feel as real as the breath within my body.

Even my dreams have changed, because where fear once held control, freedom now exists, and I have flown high above everything that once kept me grounded in fear, carried by something stronger than anything that once tried to break me, riding on the back of my dragon, Néimare, in a way that once would have felt impossible to believe and now feels like truth.

The fight to survive has ended.

Living has begun.

And for the first time in my life, I understand what it means to feel whole, not because everything is perfect, and not because every question has been answered, but because I have come into a place within myself where I no longer feel separated from who I am.

And if this path has taught me anything worth sharing, then let this be the truth that remains with you, because if I could find my way through everything I have lived, if I could reach this place after all those years of darkness, then that same possibility exists for you.

Not as a promise built on words.

But as a truth that lives within you, waiting to be seen.

"Me today."

"It took me many years to realize that I was never trapped in darkness.
I was simply inside the cocoon."

— Margaret M.R. Mechler

"You can survive this too."

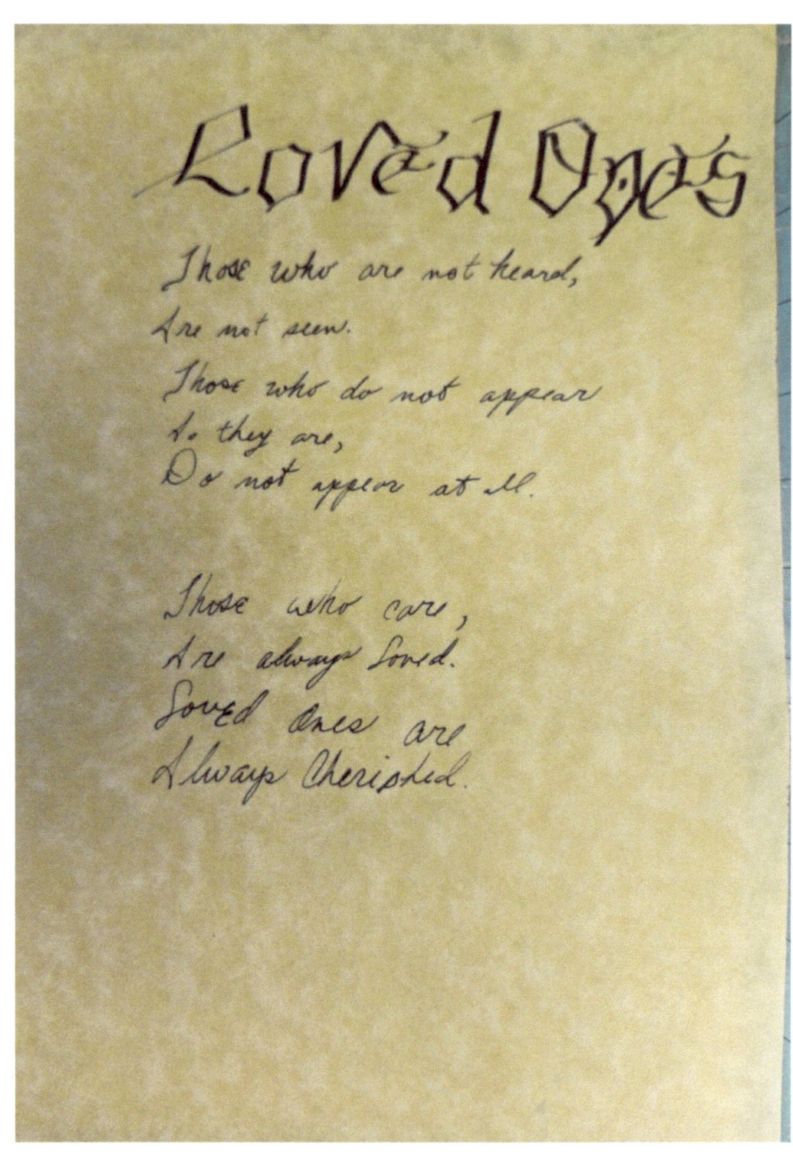
Loved Ones
Those who are not heard,
Are not seen.
Those who do not appear
As they are,
Do not appear at all.
Those who care,
Are always Loved.
Loved Ones are
Always Cherished.

www.ingramcontent.com/pod-product-compliance
Lightning Source LLC
LaVergne TN
LVHW052304100826
845147LV00006B/668

9781971169071